BREAKING
THE
TV
HABIT

BREAKING
THE
TV
HABIT

Joan
Anderson
Wilkins

CHARLES SCRIBNER'S SONS
NEW YORK

Copyright © 1982 Joan Anderson Wilkins

Library of Congress Cataloging in Publication Data

Wilkins, Joan Anderson.
  Breaking the TV habit.
  "A four-week program to help you and your
family gain control of your television viewing."
                          — Cover
  Bibliography: p.
  Includes index.
  1. Television viewers—Psychology. 2. Tele-
vision—Psychological aspects. I. Title.
II. Title: Breaking the T.V. habit.
PN1992.6.W48   1982   791.43′01′3   82-10671
ISBN 0-684-17788-9

Portions of this book have appeared, in
substantially different form, in The TV Guide-
Away © Joan Anderson Wilkins 1979.
Portions of "The Dangers of Television"
appeared, in substantially different form, in
Health © Joan Anderson Wilkins 1981

For Robin

CONTENTS

ACKNOWLEDGMENTS

The seed of this book and the concept of the Four-Week Program were planted by my husband, Robin Wilkins, a media expert and critic of the electronic environment. Nourishment for the concept of less television came from the Green Meadow Waldorf School in Spring Valley, New York, where the prevailing philosophy is that television works against the education of a child.

I owe a professional debt to those who encouraged me to develop my craft—Arthur Hettich of *Family Circle*, who gave me my start, Dan Masterson, Sam Draper, and Linda Peterson. Special help came from Everett Leonard.

Special thanks to Harvey Chertok for meeting all my deadlines, Frank Stankus, who pointed to valuable research material, and Pam Borman for her foresight and timing.

My gratitude goes to Maron Waxman, my editor, whose speed and expertise made this project take form and character in record time.

Above all, I am indebted to my children, Andrew and Luke, who continue to support the No-TV cause, and my parents, Joyce and Allan Anderson, who never permitted television to get in the way of family life.

Finally I am deeply grateful to both the Hawes and Glen Elementary Schools in Ridgewood, New Jersey, for their interest, enthusiasm, and commitment to the No-TV Week concept and to all the families and teachers who welcomed me into their homes for valuable research interviews. I have quoted extensively from these interviews in the pages that follow without further attribution. The sources for general statements in the text will be found in the Bibliography.

Joan Anderson Wilkins
Pearl River, New York

BREAKING
THE
TV
HABIT

1
THE DAY
THE TV DIED

It was lunchtime, May 24, 1974. The kids were screaming for their peanut butter and jelly sandwiches, and I was racing around the kitchen trying to get lunch over with in time for my favorite soap opera. Groceries were being strewn everywhere as three-year-old Luke was going through all the bags in search of his favorite junk cereal.

As usual, the television was on. Someone from McDonald's was telling us, "We do it all for you." At that hysterical moment I was thinking McDonald's doesn't do a damn thing for me, when all of a sudden, bam! There was a loud crash. I spun around, jelly dripping from my fingers, and there on the floor lay our portable color television set. In one puff of smoke we found ourselves televisionless. Gone was five hundred dollars;

1

gone was the next episode of "Search for Tomorrow"; and, most important of all, gone was the children's entertainment.

Poor little Luke cried the loudest because he was the one who had tripped over the cord. Andrew, our older son, and I sat down on the kitchen floor, stunned. To a family of four, who every morning greeted Captain Kangaroo and every evening said goodnight to Johnny Carson, this was a crushing blow.

For a while, a few days anyway, we walked around in a daze. I pleaded with my husband to bring a set home from the office. Since he has a job in educational communications, he had easy access to media equipment. But his excuse was that there was nothing available. Actually, I felt his trust in our ability to take care of things had diminished considerably with the breaking of the TV.

In an effort to survive, we dragged out the old black-and-white set, but television proved much less attractive in black and white than in living color.

The loss of the color television set was most devastating to me. It had taken me so very long to get the boys interested in "Sesame Street." Neither of them had ever wanted to sit still very long, but I had persevered, placing their little table and chairs right near the set and giving them snacks to eat and television toys to play with. My scheme worked. The children soon became glued to the images before them, and I was free to get on with my life. Now, however, with the loss of the TV set, I felt my freedom slipping away too.

Life without television was an entirely new experience for the children, and they rallied around almost as if they had been waiting for this day. Their first course of action was to move their table and chairs to the garage, where construction began on a tool bench. Our home, once melodic with Juicy Fruit gum ads and Kermit the Frog singing, "I like being green," suddenly resounded with hammers hammering, doors slamming, and neighborhood children giggling.

"Hmmmm," I thought to myself, "perhaps May 24 was a blessing in disguise. Perhaps life does go on in the absence of the tube."

Although we had lost a good friend in that color television set, it seemed as if ten new friends had moved in to replace it. News of the world could be heard on the radio, after all. I got reacquainted with radio talk shows. My husband and I found ourselves reading to the children at night, feeling remarkably like the parents of the Brady Bunch. In short, we suddenly found ourselves with large blocks of time that helped make our days seem longer and fuller.

Looking back now, it seems as if we stopped mourning the loss of TV rather quickly, and within weeks we made a rational decision. We would not worry where the money was coming from to replace the television. The Wilkins family was beginning to enjoy life without it! Well, almost. It actually wasn't and still isn't quite that simple. We still own a little television set; however, it is only an emaciated nine-incher that lurks in the corner of the family room, skulking under the end table. It waits there to be plucked up and turned on, and I must confess that with four people in the family it comes out of hiding for more than just a few TV specials.

Nevertheless, it remains a small innocuous creature, not a sleek and modular accessory befitting an ultramodern den and surely not something you find yourself gravitating toward. Rather, our television has become part of the family room, a bit worn at the edges like the rest of the furniture. Its face boasts a thick layer of dust. In fact, on occasion our two boys can be found drawing designs on the front of the box. And yes, even with all the video rules we have constructed, I will find the children sneaking a program in the confines of their bedroom closets. Usually they get away with it. After all, I also sneak a look at "Good Morning America" and my husband checks out "Wide World of Sports."

So what place does the television have in our household today?

We have accepted the fact that television

is here to stay. We will even go so far as to admit that it has a minimal place in the lives of our family. But for us, television will never again be our exclusive window on the world—the one place we go to for relaxation, entertainment, and information. No, we have come to realize that this electronic box transports us to unreality, showing us only what it wants us to see, when it wants us to see it, in its own contrived, clever, Technicolor way.

During our eight-year battle with the box, we have taught ourselves to be genuinely conscious of junk programming. Most of the junk gets turned off, if indeed it ever gets turned on. We used to watch "Laverne and Shirley" regularly. Then we went into one of our TV blackout periods, and the next time we flipped the show on, about a year later, we were astounded at how plastic, boring, and silly it was. Don't ask me what happened to our taste during that year. The entire family experienced the same reaction. Off went the TV, and out came the ice cream sundaes, a credible substitution, indeed.

What I'm trying to point out is that eliminating excessive television viewing in this day and age is a precarious experiment at best. This book represents eight years of trial and error during which the Wilkins family and other families following my program have gone with, gone without, and gone back to watching a lot of TV now and again. We have read all the literature critical of television, taken part in experiments to ban television, and chosen to watch only educational channels. Finally, I have conducted No-TV Week programs in public schools as well as designed workshops for parents and children to control the television problem.

Through all this, many families feel they have gained control of their television viewing and, in doing so, have gained control of how they live their lives. The Wilkins family no longer "shops where America shops," "brushes with Colgate," and "looks for the union label" whenever we go to the store. Mattel and Kenner no longer dominate our Christmases, and no well-groomed anchor interprets the news for us. Our family has developed a critical eye as well as a sense of discipline where the ON button is concerned.

Also, we are very wary about this electronic window, realizing that it connects us to nothing except, in the words of the writer Michael Arlen, the assumption of being connected to something. And finally, we believe what former *New York Times* television critic John Leonard has to say about the medium.

Although television is not taken very seriously, it should be. Five hours a day, sixty hours a week for millions, television is merging with the environment. After all, the average 16 year old has clocked more hours with the tube than he has spent in school. The TV *Guide outsells every other magazine in the nation.*

It would seem that television, which grew up to be what it is today by accident, without long-range planning, has done something in the process, also by accident, to the nation. Just as our car culture, our restless motoring, required drive-in restaurants and fast food franchises . . . filling stations of the stomach . . . so our developing TV culture requires fast food distraction, junk entertainment, psychic beef patties. The living room has been converted into a kind of car: the TV screen is its windshield; every home is mobile; everybody is in the driver's seat; and we are all seeing the same sights simultaneously.[1]

If you are convinced that gaining control of your television viewing will give you more control over your life, this book will help you. It is intended to aid parents limit the amount of television their children watch. There are many books exposing the evils of television and suggesting that children watch only a few hours a week, but none of these books give families alternatives to life with less television. Because of the medium's powerful effect, removing television, even minimally, is not an easy task. Parents need guidelines to assist them. This book will supply those guidelines, as well as a wealth of activities, projects, and strategies for every member of the family.

The first step in coming to grips with the television in your home is understanding the dangers of the TV habit, which I define as more than twelve hours of viewing a week.

The Four-Week No-TV Program described in Chapter 5 will assist you in developing a conscience about your television habit and then help you to break that habit. After following the four-week plan you will be able to evaluate the role of television in your family's life and create your own program of selective viewing with plenty of free time for other interests and activities.

After all, reports Urie Bronfenbrenner, "the primary danger of the TV screen lies *not so much in the behavior it produces as in the behavior it prevents:* the talks, the games, the family activities and the arguments through which much of the child's learning takes place and his or her own character is formed" (emphasis added).[2]

Notes

1.   "Reflections on My Seven Years at Sword's Point," *New York Times*, April 17, 1977.

2.   Quoted by Kenneth Keniston, *All Our Children—The American Family Under Pressure*, Harcourt Brace Jovanovich, 1977, p. 54.

2
TV'S IMPRINT ON OUR LIVES

Twenty-eight-year-old Susan and her husband live with their two preschool children in a small apartment. There is little sense of community in the suburb they live in, and Susan is basically alone to cope with her complicated domestic life. By three o'clock on any given day she has had it, and the television, which has been her companion for part of the day, is given over to her four-year-old daughter. Susan needs relief, and the TV set provides it for her.

Judy, the mother of two school-age children, has recently been divorced. She has a full-time job, and after school her children watch television until she comes home at five. Judy feels guilty about this, but at least she knows where her children are and what they are doing. Because she has dinner to cook and chores to do and because she is tired, the television stays on into the evening.

"So what?" you might ask. "Television is here to stay, and a little bit of viewing isn't going to hurt anyone."

True. A little bit won't hurt. But what begins as a little bit can soon get out of hand. In fact, a 1972 report published by the Surgeon General states that the average American child watches six hours of television a day—almost as much time as he or she spends in the classroom. And some children chalk up as much as fifty-four hours of TV every week.[1]

This is strong stuff. Surveys I have conducted in several New York–New Jersey suburban areas reveal more information about television and its permeation of the middle-class American household: (1) most families own a minimum of three and a maximum of five televisions; (2) at least one set in each home is color; (3) the sets are situated in vital living areas such as the living room, kitchen, bedrooms, and family room; (4) families seldom watch television together; (5) often parents do not know what their children watch; and (6) three-quarters of the people polled in the survey would be unwilling to go without television for a week, even as an experiment.

From these simple facts it is easy to figure out the general impact that television has on the interaction between members of the average suburban family. One can begin to assume that: (1) TV is a lonely recreation. Children don't have to pick and choose programs, sharing the set with parents and siblings. With several sets in the house, a child finds one that isn't being used and turns it on; (2) Many parents, therefore, fail to monitor their children's TV intake; and (3) probably the television news is on during family mealtimes.

In the early days of television, the medium was a dessert, something families shared after dinner, after daily chores, after talk time, and after homework. But what started out as dessert in the 1950s has now become the whole meal from soup to nuts.

Television was very different during its early years. For one thing, it was "live." The programs aired blatant mistakes in front of real audiences. There was a stronger code of programming ethics. Black-and-white TV was less realistic and appealing than today's color sets. There were fewer programs and channels. As a result, viewers spent less time with television and more time pursuing other interests.

Then along came a little invention guaranteed to entice families to build their lives around the TV set—TV tables. As sets became smaller and movable, the TV table made it possible and convenient to watch during mealtimes. The industry was quick to learn that if it hooked a viewer with the news, there was a good chance he or she would stay put for the rest of the evening.

And so there grew up a generation willing and ready to take to their armchairs in place of parlor games, storytelling, and family talk sessions.

Given the facts that 98 percent of all American homes have television (a greater percentage than those that have indoor toilets), that millions of homes are now wired for cable, and that still others have been experimentally hooked up to two-way systems known as interactive television, the following statistics should not shock anyone. Americans now spend 2,300 hours in front of a television set every year.[2] Television viewing ranks second only to sleeping as the nation's number-one pastime for children.[3] What's more, according to Roger Fransecky, a psychologist and consultant to CBS, children in this country are estimated to have watched between 5- and 8,000 hours of television before they enter kindergarten.[4] There is indeed some truth to the *New Yorker* cartoon showing a husband and wife sitting beside a giant television set. He says to her, "Thirty-one years of television together . . . surely that means something!"

Television has slowly worked its way into the social fabric of the nation, resulting in silence replacing conversation, sitcoms replacing bedtime stories, and staring at the TV replacing sitting by the hearth. As John Leonard aptly put it, "Television isn't just in the environment: it is the environment."[5] To squarely face television's role in

American life, it is important to understand what the TV means in your home. It is surely more than just another electronic appliance, like the radio or stereo. Television has the ability to bring, in living color, many uninvited guests into your living room.

First, television is a *salesperson*. Most of us are pretty skeptical about the salespeople who knock at our doors or call us up with their special deals. The television set, however, constantly beams commercial messages to us day after day—350,000 by the time a child graduates from high school.[6] In many instances, the programs are secondary to the products that are being sold. After all, you can't run a program on television if it doesn't have many sponsors.

Second, television is a *teacher*. Many families choose the location of their home based on the best possible school district for their children. Further, over the school years, these same parents spend thousands of dollars educating their children. Parents constantly quiz friends and neighbors about teachers, and many handpick the best ones for their children each year. But these very same parents seem curiously unaware that when their children are not in school, many are learning from a host of anonymous teachers on television who are teaching a curriculum that is almost entirely unfamiliar to the parent. This curriculum covers every aspect of life, from the values children will follow to the jeans they will wear.

And third, television is a *companion.* After saying a quick hello to a parent or babysitter after school, many children head for the television. They spend the rest of the afternoon with a companion who doesn't talk to them, doesn't ask any questions of them, and doesn't demand any cooperation in order to play with them.

Have you ever wondered why children like their television companions so much? Look at the programs they watch. Some favorites among children are "The Brady Bunch," "Eight Is Enough," and "Different Strokes," all of which show the "typical" American family. Without any real effort— with most of the fun and little of the work —children become part of a family. But a close look at these TV families reveals that the characters on these shows never watch television. They're too busy doing the things that active, lively, normal children like to do—play games, enter contests, have slumber parties, play tricks on one another, do chores, and talk on the telephone.

Why are these shows and others like them so appealing to children? Perhaps because they provide children with a picture of family life at its best, where parents participate, people talk to one another, and living together looks like fun. In short, children get pleasure out of watching these fantasies of family life. They dream of living this kind of life if only someone would show them how. "Communication and shared activity are the most sought after experiences of youth with parents," according to a Canadian Radio-TV Telecommunications Commission.⁷ Many children recognize, in some innate way, their need to participate in their own lives and in the lives of their family. Television companions fill that need, even if vicariously.

But the late Dr. Dorothy Cohen of the Bank Street College of Education in New York City cautions parents on just this point:

> *Children need people most of all. Parents and teachers must arouse themselves from their mesmerized state and take a good look at how they are using television as a substitute for themselves, even as television uses cartoons as substitutes for the images of real people. Children cannot become human if they relate heavily to an image of an image or, at best, to a nonresponding, nontouchable image of a person.*
>
> *Children are steadily losing contact with people, as individual craftsmen, small businessmen, and good neighbors give way to impersonal big establishments. Adults cannot share their contemporary life style with children because it is not easy for children to tune into office work and complex machines.*

On top of that, parents are so rushed that they find it hard to take time for their children even if they want to.

All of society is slipping into a greater reliance on the image of the thing rather than the real thing itself. Television is no better or worse than the rest of society, but it is the major instrument by which, at present, we hasten the process of alienation in our young and interfere with the processes of ego strengthening which grow primarily through contact with reality, not images, through participation and interaction with people and things, not through passivity and imitation.[8]

There also is evidence that shows adults are affected by television. For many people television is used as an escape from the stress of everyday life. Television has become the major form of relaxation after a hard day at the office. However, a team of researchers from UCLA, headed by Roderic Gorney, found that television viewing could heighten tension and aggression rather than lessen it. In this study, 183 couples living in Los Angeles were asked to watch specific programs.[9] The shows fell into four categories: heavily violent, programs with helpful themes, light entertainment, and a mixture of all three. The men were told to choose shows from only one category and watch them exclusively for a week. Meanwhile, the women were secretly monitoring their husbands' behavior.

The results indicated changes in behavior as a result of television viewing. For instance, those who watched helpful programs such as "The Waltons" showed a marked decrease in the amount of harmful behavior and aggressive moods exhibited. They were much more likely to play with a sick child or help their children with homework. On the other hand, the men who watched violent shows remained much the same or became more aggressive. They were likely to start an argument or kick a child's toy left behind on the living room floor.

When I lead workshops many women complain to me that their husbands are so addicted to television they hardly know the family is around. Several have blamed their bad marriages on television. Lawrence Friedman, a Los Angeles psychiatrist, says, "I am convinced that at least 50 percent of all divorces in this country are unnecessary. And it's all because TV teaches us simple solutions to complex problems. People tell me: 'If only I could get rid of this marriage, everything would be all right.' Nonsense!"[10]

Other behavior problems can be blamed on television according to an Annenberg School of Communications study of adults. These findings stated that people whose viewing habits center on crime shows are more likely to buy a dog or even a gun for protection, install new locks on doors and

windows, and avoid what they consider to
be unsafe sections of town.

At this point it would be fair to ask,
"Come on now, television isn't all bad, is it?"
The answer is, of course, no.
After all, television does serve several
valuable purposes. Older persons and dis-
abled people who can't easily get out of their
homes can learn a great deal from television
and also stay in touch with the world. A
young at-home parent can see exciting
drama like "Masterpiece Theatre," as well
as pick up many "how-to's" from various
talk shows. The struggling family that can't
afford a babysitter is able to see feature-
length movies in their own living room.
Millions of people who live outside major
metropolitan areas can, if they wish, enjoy
first-rate ballet, concerts, opera, and sports
events. And all of us can be part of many
historic once-in-a-lifetime events—man's
first walk on the moon, the inauguration of
a president, the wedding of a prince and
princess.

Further, good programming does exist.
Every year the National PTA publishes a
list of recommended programs that make a
positive contribution to the quality of family life. In the past such lists have included
"Little House on the Prairie," "World of
Disney," "The Waltons," "Sixty Minutes,"
and "Eight Is Enough." The PTA is also
quick to note programs rated poor because

of violence and sex. This list has included "Soap," "Three's Company," "Kojak," "Charlie's Angels," "Starsky and Hutch," and "The Dukes of Hazzard."

It is important to note, though, that those who benefit most from TV—good television, bad television, indifferent television —are adults. Their major growth and learning may be behind them. Children, on the other hand, are growing and learning every day. It is both unfair and dangerous to cut them off from the real world before they have a chance to experience it, to rob them of their creative, intellectual, and physical resources and energies before they've had a chance to use them.

Recently, during a television lecture I was conducting, a member of the audience thought I was being unfair about television for older people. She felt strongly that the elderly had little else but television to give them a window on the world and that I shouldn't be so critical of the medium where these people were concerned. I agreed with her, but that does not answer this question: "Do we want our young people to start out their lives in the same way our senior citizens are finishing theirs out?"

Surely parents have it in their power to control their children's television viewing, but many seem to lack the energy to exercise this power. Ironically, parents feel guilty because they know about the latest studies indicating that too much television is harmful, especially to children, and yet, for one free hour, or two, or three, it seems worth it for now.

The problem then boils down to working out a way to use television and not abuse it. To successfully control television watching in your family, you must be persuaded that all family members will benefit from a program of selective viewing.

Notes

1. *Television and Social Behavior: A Technical Report to the Surgeon General's Scientific Advisory Commission on Television and Social Behavior*, 5 volumes, Washington, D.C., 1972. At this point it's difficult to say exactly how many hours the average American spends watching television or other electronic devices. In 1981, A. C. Nielsen estimated that the average American watched 29 hours and 46 minutes a week, but this figure does not include cable television or video games. According to "A Ten-Year Study of TV Violence," published by the Annenberg School of Communications in 1979, "Heavy viewers watch six hours a day. . . . The vast majority of American children approach the heavy level in their normal habitual viewing patterns." Russ Faist, "Here's How to Handle TV," *Catholic Universe Bulletin*, September 29, 1978, reports that "the average home has a lighted TV screen on six and one half hours a day" (p. 13).

2. Nielsen for percent of American homes; Faist for 2,300 hours.

3. Richard P. Adler, "Parents' Television Guide," *Learning*, December 1978.

4. Interview, *People*, October 8, 1979, p. 55.

5. "Reflections on My Seven Years at Sword's Point," *New York Times*, April 17, 1977.

6. Baltimore Media Alliance, P.O. Box 16262, Baltimore, Maryland 21210.

7. Quoted by "Parents' Television Guide," p. 5.

8. "Is TV a Pied Piper?" *Young Children Journal*, November 1974, pp. 12–13.

9. Reported in Constance Rosenblum, "Are You Only As Nice As the Show You Watch?" *New York Daily News*, June 24, 1979.

10. "Television and Values," the Learning Seed Company, teachers' guide to filmstrip, p. 15.

3
THE DANGERS OF TELEVISION

Television happened to us. We weren't prepared for its onslaught any more than we were ready for junk food that lacked nutrients, nuclear plants that leak, or survival techniques for living in the suburbs. Television invaded our homes, multiplying three-, four-, and fivefold; it imposed its morals, its values, and its way of life on us. Now it has even become a member of the family, sometimes the one we spend the most time with. What's worse, television's effects have crept up on us silently but cumulatively, to the point of affecting the entire nation.

Just as it takes several months or years for a person to gain excess weight, so it also takes months or years of excessive TV viewing for video residue to build in human beings. Therefore, television's harmful effects are not always readily visible. The dangers of television, however, actually begin very early in life. Neil Postman, a professor of communications at New York University who has written extensively on the effects of television, contends, "The medium of television becomes intelligible to children beginning at about thirty-six months. From this very early age on, television continuously exerts influence."[1] Infants within earshot of a turned-on television set do not seem to notice or react to the machine. However, when these children begin to utter sounds, the language may be garbled, as the children mimic the sounds they have heard—video sounds. "Children learn to speak by talking to real people, not by listening to mechanically reproduced speech. Real people speaking communicate the meaning of words, whereas television only reproduces sounds, a subtle but vital difference, confusing for toddlers," reports the Association of Assistant School Mistresses.[2]

Later these children enter kindergarten with letter and number recognition under their belts; along about third or fourth grade, however, when asked to write words they know, string thoughts together, and think creatively and expansively, many of these children fall short because they have learned to understand only pictures and words spoken by others. Over the years these children have become clones of TV characters, even adopting their physical motions and speech patterns. When they become teens, these children exhibit the residual effects of television even more apparently. Many lack the ability to cope and to express themselves verbally. Often, TV teens have a set of values dictated largely by Hollywood grownups.

Now that television has been part of our lives for forty years, critics and researchers have begun to analyze the effects it has on us and on our family life.

In 1977, Marie Winn, the author of several books for parents and children, wrote a widely discussed work called *The Plug-In Drug*, based on interviews about the television-viewing habits of middle-class families in New York City and Denver. In the book she contends that television has led to a decline in reading and writing skills, a diminution of socializing experiences, fragmentation of the nuclear family, a rise in drug use, an increase in overactive behavior, and the creation of a breed of remorseless children.

The 1972 *Surgeon General's Report on Television and Social Behavior*, which had anticipated many of Winn's arguments, concludes that television viewing has contributed to the disappearance of conversation, correspondence, and visits to friends' homes. Apparent permanent casualties of television viewing are sleeping (TV addicts sleep less), listening to the radio, and reading books. Television children, the report states, tend to be passive, bashful, and easily distracted.

Pediatricians, responding to a poll conducted by the American Medical Association, blamed exposure to television violence for heightened aggression in children, epileptic seizures, nightmares, and injuries resulting from emulating TV incidents. Nearly 14 percent of the responding 147 physicians said they had seen patients with behavioral and physical problems which may be related to television violence. Another 41 percent said that they "suspect so."[3]

Teachers are also beginning to find disturbing symptoms. After interviewing teachers along the eastern seaboard, Nancy Larrick reported in *The New York Times* that television children are tired when they get to school from too much watching the previous night or before school in the morning, that they have a glazed, staring quality about their eyes, and that they are either extremely overactive or extremely apathetic.

Television research centers at such universities as Yale, Harvard, UCLA, and the University of Pennsylvania's Annenberg School of Communications continue to measure and quantify TV's effects. Joining them in the search for answers to these questions and plans for control are the National PTA, the American Medical Association, and various religious organizations. Their observa-

tions and criticisms center on the following
major areas of concern.

Weakened Powers of Imagination

Vital to children is the ability to make
up their own pictures and to explore the
world of newly created fantasies—in short,
to be given the opportunity to use their
imaginations. Television children are being
denied that right and, consequently, have
lost some of their imaginative powers. Their
play is not creative or imaginative. Television children copy TV superheroes, according to Ann Stahl, a nursery school
teacher at the private Green Meadow Waldorf School in Spring Valley, New York.
(The Waldorf philosophy is that children
learn by doing, thinking and playing—and,
therefore, not by watching TV.) "You'll see
children standing on top of tables with
towels and aprons wrapped around their
necks, imitating Batman. They do a lot of
aimless running, punching, and shouting.
It's very hard to interest TV children in
listening to a story, or in anything else, for
that matter. Their references, speech patterns, and words sound like a recording of
a TV show." Girls, Ann Stahl says, are exceptionally skillful at mimicking the characters they see on television.

Children have always taken on the roles
of their favorite heroes or characters in
play—there's nothing new there. But close

observers of heavy TV-viewers say that these children aren't adding anything original or imaginative to their game of, let's say, "Star Trek." They know the layout of the starship *Enterprise*. And they know, from having logged hours and hours of listening, exactly how Captain Kirk and Mr. Spock and all the others should sound. In their play, they simply reenact what they've seen the evening before. Lying dormant is the imagination, the food that nourishes and stimulates the young mind.

Rarely do these children get to experience the hard work that comes into play when they are forced to create pictures during the process of reading a book or listening to the radio. It was in books that the televisionless child of yesteryear had to "picture" the witch or "picture" the hero, calling upon his or her own unique imaginative powers to do the job.

Unimaginative children of television sometimes even forget to play. A mother of two girls explained it this way, "They sit around and wait for their TV shows to begin while their toy closet stands untouched and neat. When they do play, their activity consists of jumping from one thing to another, making a huge mess and then, in twenty minutes or so, walking away from the mayhem. I don't think they know how to play any more."

Many people argue that television programs stimulate the imagination by expos-

ing children to things they might not otherwise see or hear. Perhaps, on occasion, this
occurs, especially when a child watches an
educational show. But for the most part,
TV feeds the viewer, young and old, information that is thoroughly "predigested." In
most cases, little is demanded of the viewer
in response or reaction—quite simply, he is
not even asked to "chew."

Harvard University researchers, in a
study called Project Zero, concluded that
how a person received information made a
difference in how the brain was able to use
it. Howard Gardner, the project director,
believes "Television children rarely go beyond the picture language either to pay
attention to the audio portion or to connect
TV experiences to their own real life experiences."[4] The project also found that children
not only have better recall of stories read to
them than of stories they see on television
but that they also recall the language of a
read story more precisely. It seems that
children show a greater tendency to inte-
grate their own experiences into a read story
as well as draw inferences from it.

Do movies have the same damaging effects as television on a child's imagination?
There are some positive aspects of going to
the movies that outweigh the negatives.
When you take a child to the movies (or go
yourself), it is not a passive, isolated experience. It's an excursion outside the home,
during which there is an opportunity to so-

cialize with family and friends. It also offers an opportunity for discussion on the way home. Moreover, you have chosen to see a specific picture at a particular time instead of merely being a passive recipient of whatever happens to be on the tube.

Exposure to Violence and Other Inappropriate Subject Matter and Language

Everyone has seen little children go "bang-bang" at each other and fall down dead when they are shot. These children have probably never witnessed a shooting— at least not in real life. Psychologists believe that violence is a learned behavior, and scientific evidence reveals that children do indeed learn the violence from television.

A study done by Dr. Albert Bandura, a psychologist at Stanford University, demonstrated rather effectively how violent actions seen on television are taken up by the children who watch them. Dr. Bandura set up two control groups of youngsters. Group one viewed a video tape of a grownup hitting, pushing, punching, and eventually sitting on top of an inflated life-sized rubber doll. After viewing the tape, the children were given a similar doll, and they proceeded to treat the doll precisely as they saw it being treated on television.

Group two did not see the video tape. Instead, they were taken to a room in which there was a similar doll. Their treatment of the doll was original and lacked violent actions.[5]

Given the fact that the average viewer sees eight major acts of violence an hour— not including reruns of violent cartoons, police shows, verbal violence, and all the "funny" hitting, pushing, and driving of cars off cliffs—one has to assume that eventually there will be effects from this exposure, and there has been.[6] Ten years after the Surgeon General's report on television and social behavior, the National Institute of Mental Health reviewed the data and studies that had been published since 1970 and concluded, "The consensus among most of the research community is that violence on television does lead to aggressive behavior by children and teenagers who watch the programs. . . . In magnitude, television violence is as strongly correlated with aggressive behavior as any other behavioral variant that has been measured."[7] Four theories were advanced in support of the link between television and violence: (1) observational learning (children learn by seeing), (2) attitude change (television makes children distrustful of the world), (3) arousal (children are physiologically aroused by watching violence on television), and (4) justification (the violence and aggression of television heroes justify the aggressiveness of children who watch television).

A study by ABC indicates that 22 percent of crimes committed by juveniles are suggested by TV programs. In 1981 a nine-year-old boy accused of robbing a New York City bank with a toy gun was defended by his lawyer with the argument that the child got the idea from watching television. In another incident a fourteen-year-old shot and killed his younger brother while reenacting a scene from the movie *Dirty Harry*. Daniel Schorr, senior Washington correspondent for Cable News Network, sees John Hinckley, accused of trying to assassinate President Reagan, as a "media freak," a young man who spent thousands of hours watching television alone. Schorr reports that in written replies to *Newsweek*, Hinckley stated that watching so much television was "quite dangerous." Commenting on the coverage the assassination attempt was receiving, Hinckley, though pleased, said, "That's too bad, because it's going to affect other people."[8]

Cases of TV-inspired violence are not always this dramatic; an eight-year-old boy told me that the bad thing about television is "we begin to think we can solve problems with fist fights, like they do on TV." Dr. Charles Atkins and Dr. Bradley Greenberg, of the Department of Communications at Michigan State University, have studied children in the sixth through eighth grades. "We've analyzed how kids behave in an aggressive fashion on a day-to-day basis, and we've found those who watched violent shows gave more aggressive answers on how to solve day-to-day problems."[9]

A further negative aspect of the effect of television violence on children was revealed in a 1979 survey conducted by the Foundation for Child Development in New York City. Results showed that heavy-viewing children were more fearful of the world and more likely to have bad dreams than children who saw less television. This is not surprising, considering that by the time a steady viewer has reached the age of fourteen, he or she will have witnessed over 11,000 television murders.[10]

In 1979 the Annenberg School of Communications report "A Ten-Year Study of TV Violence" confirmed that schoolchildren who were steady TV viewers had an exaggerated sense of danger and mistrust compared with children who watched only small amounts. The study also found that television children are more likely to believe the police frequently use force and will shoot fleeing suspects.

How does television violence differ from the violence in traditional fairy tales, which are filled with gory incidents and terrifying villains? For one thing, most children view TV violence while they are alone. Their parents or babysitters are often in another part of the house while monsters, murderers, and various other brutes are entertaining the child. The child takes in the fear but has no way to channel his or her anguish or trepidation. A fairy tale, on the other hand, is usually read to a youngster while he or she is sitting on mom or dad's lap, all nice and safe. When there is a scary moment, it is cloaked in the warmth of a parent's voice. Questions can be answered and mysteries can be solved as they occur. Fears can be allayed and, more importantly, there is communication between two human beings.

Television violence not only encourages similar violence and scares children; it can also desensitize them. To extinguish unwanted and antisocial emotions in troubled people, psychologists use a technique called imaginal desensitization. With imagery and fantasy materials psychologists strip their patients of these feelings until they can remain relaxed and unperturbed when confronted with situations that initially caused them distress. Television works much the same way with its steady stream of brutality.[11]

Erma Bombeck sums this up in her own special way. She once wrote an angry letter to the networks that went like this: "During a single evening I saw twelve people shot, two tortured, one dumped into a swimming pool, two cars explode, a rape, and a man who crawled two blocks with a knife in his stomach. Do you know something? I didn't feel anger or shock or horror or excitement or repugnance. The truth is I didn't feel. Through repeated assaults of one violent act after another, you have taken from me some-

thing I valued—something that contributed
to my compassion and caring—the instinct
to feel."[12] This was brought home to me by
a mother who remarked, "It's really amazing what happens when the kids and I watch
an emotional television program. I start to
cry as soon as the mood begins to get senti-
mental, and the kids all turn around and
watch me. . . . After seeing thousands of
hours of televised emotion, the kids seem to
be immune."

Television also introduces into our
homes a whole range of subjects and language usually considered inappropriate for
children. "What television does is bring a
whole culture out of the closet, because programs need such a constant supply of information," says Professor Postman. "In its
quest for new and sensational ventures to
hold its audience, TV must tap every exist-
ing taboo in the culture—homosexuality,
incest, divorce, promiscuity, corruption,
adultery, and terrible displays of violence
and sadism. As a consequence, these become
as familiar to the young as to adults."[13]

The television explosion has also
changed our language. It seems logical that
if children's sheets, dishes, T-shirts, and
underwear are covered with television characters, the words popping out of their
mouths will be the language of their TV
peers. Many kindergartners shout angrily
to friends, "If you don't stop, I'm going to
divorce you." "They talk about screwing,

being gay, and blowing up the world, and all these subjects are sprinkled with TV vernacular," reports a teacher from West-chester, a New York City suburb. "The younger children barely comprehend what they are saying, and the older children, it seems to me, know too soon the meanings of words and subjects that are better left for explanation later in their lives. Personally, I think it's sad."

Extremely Apathetic or Overactive Behavior

Perhaps the worst time of the week for parents is Saturday morning, when Mommy tries to coax Johnny away from the cartoons and outdoors to play. She calls to him several times, but to no avail. Finally, in frustration, she shouts, "Johnny, turn off that TV!" Johnny slowly turns his freckled face in her direction, tries to focus his glazed eyes, and answers, "Do I have to?" Angry conversation follows, with Johnny becoming more cranky and miserable by the minute. Clearly no one is going to win at this game.

Part of the problem may be that Johnny has been jarred out of an alpha state; his brain waves are in a pattern that indicates deep relaxation. According to a study for General Electric by sociologist Herbert E. Krugman, after a very short span of time (sometimes as little as thirty seconds) a television watcher's brain waves go into an alpha pattern.[14] This implies that when a child is called away from television after a heavy dose of viewing, he or she is being awakened from a pseudo-nap in which his or her "dreams" have consisted of the ingredients dished up in cartoons—noise, ugly and frightening characters, frantic music, violence. It should come as no surprise that the child is grouchy and irritable.

At the other extreme, some children are simply overstimulated after being bombarded by all of television's sensory impressions. Dr. Werner I. Halpern of the Rochester Mental Health Clinic reported a sudden increase in the number of two-year-olds being referred to the clinic for behavioral problems.[15] They were restless, hyperactive, and frantic and exhibited other problems, such as inappropriate speech, that contained a great deal of compulsive serializing of letters and numbers. These children found it easier to relate to things than to people. A battery of tests revealed that the children were not psychotic, autistic, or schizophrenic. Dr. Halpern concluded that watching television, particularly "Sesame Street," was the one thing all of the children were exposed to. When the children stopped watching television, their symptoms disappeared and their behavior improved rapidly.

Another more simple-minded answer for the overactive child seems obvious. It is not natural for active, young human beings to stay in a sitting position and stare at a box for hours. Therefore, when the television goes off after several hours of watching, children are bound to be wild, loud, and busy. Could it be that the youngsters are simply making up for the time spent being idle and contained?

Confusion of Real Life with TV Life

At a recent meeting of the New York Council for Children's Television, teachers reported that first, second, and third graders assume much of what they see on television to be real and true. One teacher, explaining how her class was terribly upset after seeing the TV version of *Jaws*, said "The children were convinced that the shark was real, that the situation happened, that the man had been swallowed up by a real shark and killed. I allowed them to tell me stories and to draw and paint pictures of what they had seen. The discussions continued all day, but I had no luck convincing them that *Jaws* was just a show."

My own son Luke watched a made-for-television movie of *Salem's Lot*, without my knowing it. For some time thereafter he refused to go to bed without a light on in his room, the hallway, and the bathroom. Six months went by and I was still waiting for this "stage" to pass. Quite casually one day I asked both boys if there was anything that really scared them. "Oh yes," said Luke

matter-of-factly. "I'm scared of Barlow."
"Who's Barlow?" I asked. "The vampire on
Salem's Lot," he replied. "That's why I'm
scared to go to sleep at night."

Children need parents to explain the
mysteries that the television box holds for
them. Children's fears come alive at bedtime, and many are a direct result of television. One preschooler I met was afraid to
go to sleep because she thought the "green
eyes" would get her. Her mother took all
the steps that comfort children. She looked
under the bed, in the closet, and inside the
drawers declaring that no green eyes were
to be found. But the child persevered. "Yes,
Mommy, the green eyes are in the box."
"What box?" her mother asked. "The television box!" answered her daughter. The
child had seen a TV commercial for a horror
movie in which there was a witch with green
eyes; quite naturally, this five year old
thought that all the creatures on the screen
lived in the box.

A little boy in upstate New York was
watching a war movie one day that featured
a chase scene with World War II airplanes.
Suddenly his mother heard a loud crash. She
ran into the room to see her son standing
next to a broken television screen. The boy
looked up in a daze and explained that he
only wanted to see where the airplane had
gone.

It is surely safe to suggest that children
who view more television than real life be-

gin to believe that reality is what they see on television.

Adopting of Television Values

For centuries children have been raised with the values and traditions of their families. Television has changed much of that by creating its own set of values and, many times in the process, superimposing these values on today's family. "The Brady Bunch," for example, are always a happy group, and that's a pretty abnormal situation for most families. "Dallas," on the other hand (a favorite show of grade-school children), highlights greed, white-collar crime, and sex, making it very attractive and entertaining. Cops and robbers shows dole out a message that says it's all right to solve problems by beating and shooting. Television shows underrepresent old people and minorities, and women are always beautiful.

An impressionable young viewer is quite likely to take these video values for his own. The NIMH report stresses the role of television as a powerful and pervasive educator that has become "a major socializing agent of American children."[16]

What do children gain from a weekend spent with their parents? Teachers at the First Presbyterian Pre-School, a nursery school in Englewood, New Jersey, report that when they ask their students what they did over a long weekend, most children describe only the shows they watched on television. Even with additional prodding and probing, most children find it difficult to remember other activities. Perhaps the children went to church, visited a relative, or went to the grocery store, but all these activities fade when compared to television activity.

Rose Goldsen, a frequent critic of television, expressed her concern this way:

> *So thoroughly has television saturated the environment we make and share with one another, that nearly every child born in this country is inescapably immersed in its symbols during the most formative years of infancy and childhood. What will happen to the body movements and body rhythms of these children, their facial expressions and their emotive use of language, their dreams, their fancies, and their fantasies? Will all converge toward some Universal Mean? What are the symbols that will then call forth their allegiance, devotion, and reverential love?*[17]

Interference with True Learning

Television is often considered a learning tool, and when it is used in the classroom setting, where a teacher prepares the children before, during, and after a program, it can be effective. But remember that television is mostly vision. I recently recorded a twenty-minute segment of "Sixty Minutes" to get information for an article I was writing. When the tape was transcribed, I had only one-half page of typewritten words. Even documentaries are not full of factual information; they are full of visual impressions.

Professor Postman explains TV learning this way: "Television can never teach what a medium like a book can teach, and yet educators are always trying to pretend that they can use TV to promote the cognitive habits and the intellectual discipline that print promotes. Television is not a suitable medium for conveying ideas because an idea is essentially language—words and sentences."[18]

Sheila Nielsen, a teacher at the Waldorf School in Spring Valley, New York, points out another obstacle television throws up in the path of learning. "Because most programs run seven minutes, then break for commercials, television children are programmed for concentration spans of seven minutes." These children are not learning how to immerse themselves in absorbing thought. They are learning that they have as many options for quick, easy entertainment as there are channels on the set. Even though many teachers know the children are theoretically capable of much longer spans of attention, in today's classrooms they must now schedule activities so that the subject or pace changes every seven minutes. Otherwise, they lose the children's attention.

Dr. Mary Alice White, a professor of psychology and education at Teachers College of Columbia University, cites the same problem:

> By the time they are three or four years old, children have learned that music and sound effects, and sometimes changes in types of voices, are cues to make them look at a TV screen. They come to school with a set of strategies they have learned from the electronic system that do not apply to the classroom setting. I don't think they know when to listen.[19]

The New York Times reported on March 30, 1982, studies that indicate a relation between heavy TV viewing and low achievement scores. Although researchers are not saying that television causes low achievement, a project conducted by the California Department of Education found that sixth graders who watched "B.J. and the Bear," "The Incredible Hulk," and "Dance Fever" scored lower on standard achievement tests than students who did not. Many of the low-scoring students watched six hours of television a night, whereas many of the students who watched less television and programs of better quality scored higher.

A University of Toronto study indicated that television shrinks a child's chance to learn. Researchers there showed that the vocabulary used on television is narrower than that used in children's books, and that TV's dominant form of communication is the incomplete sentence.

But what about educational television? Many parents think that if their children watch anything, it should be "Sesame Street." Surely there can't be anything wrong with watching "Sesame Street"?

To answer this question, it is important to understand the history of "Sesame Street." This program came into being as a gallant effort to bring basic learning skills to the culturally deprived and disadvantaged child. The Children's Television Workshop set out to teach letters and numbers to these youngsters so they would be ready for the task at hand when they eventually reached kindergarten. The methods to reach them were modeled on the TV commercial and TV rhyme for it was believed that these children were heavy TV viewers. By selling letters and numbers the way television sells toothpaste and toys, the creators of "Sesame Street" hoped to reach their audience. No one could have predicted that "Sesame

Street" would take off in such a phenomenal way. In fact, it was never intended to be watched as frequently as it currently is, nor was the format designed for children under the age of three.

Exposure to the Madison Avenue techniques of fast-paced pictures and images, high-speed action, quick sell, varied color, heightened volume, and many animated characters, which are the techniques of television in general, has had a startling effect on many young children, and on the culture of childhood. The effects have been maximized partially because of the availability of the program. In most towns across the country "Sesame Street" can be viewed three times on Saturday, six times on Sunday, and four times daily during the week. Most children don't actively watch the show during all these time slots, but many have adopted the "Sesame Street" family as their own and therefore seem to derive comfort from the program even if just for background noise and companionship.

Being continually and explosively bombarded with such TV techniques, preschool children begin to show problem signs from taking in so many sensory impressions. As mentioned earlier, Dr. Halpern believes that watching "Sesame Street" creates sensory overload in some very young children. He also feels that the rapid changes and choppiness of movement prevent reflection on the part of the child. This is destructive because it hinders a child's adaptive capacity and disturbs the balance of the child's inner life. Overloading the sensory receptors breeds a sense of powerlessness. There are children who cannot deal with many new sensory impressions all at once, and "Sesame Street" provides neither the time nor the repetition these children need to reflect on these stimuli and thereby digest and truly learn the material. It is important to note that, since Dr. Halpern's study, the producers of "Sesame Street" have slowed down portions of the program in an effort to guard against sensory overload. The original quick style for letters and numbers remains, though.

Jerome L. Singer and Dorothy G. Singer, a Yale University husband and wife team who head up a television research center, are struck by the fact that even though children pay close attention to "Sesame Street," the rapid pace and constant intrusion of new material seem to interfere with effective learning. "In some of our studies," the Singers report, "we found that children benefit more from slower-paced programs like 'Mr. Rogers' Neighborhood.' As with a good children's book, Mr. Rogers allows a child time to savor the material. We have found that after viewing Mr. Rogers for a few weeks, the children become more imaginative, more cooperative, smile, and concentrate more than the child who has watched 'Sesame Street' for the same period of time."[20]

But "Sesame Street" does teach children something. Dr. Dorothy Cohen noted that children who watched "Sesame Street" learned number and letter recognition, but she questioned whether they internalized what they saw. Rose Goldsen asserts that "Sesame Street" teaches children to read television, not books. "They also learn a new sense of time," she continues. "The fragmented hour and the fifty-four-minute hour become the child's new sense of timing." Goldsen also reports that the "Sesame Street" curriculum has nothing to do with books or with the culture of books. "Not one episode," she points out, "has a book. No one on 'Sesame Street' is shown absorbed in a book, laughing or crying over a book, or so gripped by a book that he cannot put it down. Given the stated intention of 'Sesame Street' to encourage an interest in literature, its failure to push books may seem contradictory."[21]

There is also a vital difference between even the best of television programs and a book or a magazine. There is no way to stop the action on a television program and ask for explanation of a confusing point. There's no way to question a dubious assumption and no way to reread a difficult passage. In a book, a child can always turn back to a favorite page and look at it again. A story can be enjoyed at the child's own pace. When watching television, a child has to keep TV's pace whether or not it's suited to him or her. How can learning possibly take place in any but a superficial way?

And finally, psychologist Urie Bronfenbrenner asks the question: In addition to learning about language, numbers, and reasoning what else is left scrawled on a child's psyche from watching "Sesame Street"?

- Children will imitate certain physical acts, such as those shown in slapstick episodes.
- Sweet and unhealthy foods are glorified by Cookie Monster, and his sloppy eating habits will be imitated.
- "Sesame Street" keeps children from getting "out in the backyard breathing God's good air, so their bodies can grow healthy and strong" in Francis Kelly's words.
- The series teaches poor grammar and vocabulary.
- Children will acquire a false attitude that learning always will be fun and not the serious, tedious business that it really is.[22]

A famous theologian once said, "Give me a child until he is seven, and I will have him for life." Is television the teacher we want to shape our children's lives?

Notes

1. Neil Postman, "TV's Disastrous Impact on Children," *U.S. News & World Report*, January 19, 1981, pp. 43–46.

2. "The Teaching of Reading," cited in "Television and Child Development," a pamphlet from the TV Action Group, Schoolhouse, Brookthorpe, Gloucester, Massachusetts.

3. *American Medical News*, June 20, 1979.

4. Quoted by Kate Moody, "The Research on TV—A Disturbing Picture," *New York Times Spring Survey of Education*, April 20, 1980.

5. Albert Bandura, D. Ross, and S. A. Ross, "Imitation of Film-Mediated Aggressive Models," *Journal of Abnormal and Social Psychology*, 1963, p. 8. The article is discussed in the Learning Seed Company's teachers' guide to the filmstrip *Television Violence*.

6. National Coalition on Television Violence for the period January 4–March 27, 1982. In 1979, George Gerbner, coprincipal investigator for an Annenberg School of Communications study, put the figure at 15.6 violent acts in 1977 and 25 in 1978.

7. David Pearl, director, *Television and Behavior: 10 Years of Scientific Progress and Implications for the Eighties*, Washington, D.C., 1982.

8. ABC study cited in Warren Weaver, Jr., "A Court Ruling Lets Child Victim of Sex Assault Sue a TV Network," *New York Times*,

April 25, 1978; robbery, E. R. Shipp, "Armed Robbery Is Court Charge Faced by Boy, Nine," *New York Times*, March 8, 1981; Schorr, "Hinckley: A 'Media Freak,' " *New York Times*, May 10, 1982.

9. Quoted by John Mariani, "The Impact of TV Violence on Your Children," *Family Weekly*, November 11, 1979, p. 32.

10. Baltimore Media Alliance, P.O. Box 16262, Baltimore, Maryland 21210.

11. Rose Goldsen, in *The Show and Tell Machine —How Television Works and Works You Over*, Delta, 1978 (page 10), cites the work of the psychologists H. R. Beech and H. J. Eysenck in this connection.

12. "Let Children Feel Compassion; Curb Television Violence," *Journal News* (Rockland County, New York).

13. "TV's Disastrous Impact on Children," p. 45.

14. "Brain Waves Measures of Media Involvement," *Journal of Advertising Research*, February 1971, pp. 66–70.

15. "Turned-on Toddlers—Effects of Television on Children and Adolescents," *Journal of Communications*, Autumn 1975, p. 70.

16. *Television and Behavior*.

17. *The Show and Tell Machine*, p. 63.

18. "TV's Disastrous Impact on Children," p. 43.

19. *TC Today* (Newsletter of Teachers College, Columbia University), Fall 1981, n. p.

20. "Is Human Imagination Going Down the Tube?" *Chronicles of Higher Education,* April 23, 1979.

21. *The Show and Tell Machine,* 250–251.

22. "Who Lives on Sesame Street?" *Psychology Today,* October 1970, pp. 14–18.

4
WHO IS
THE VID-KID?

It's interesting to ask people how many hours of television they watch a day. Television watching is like eating peanuts or pretzels or chocolate-chip cookies. You quickly lose count of what you have consumed. Television is in every house. Sometimes there's a set in every room; sometimes a set is turned on just for background noise or company. It's impossible for most of us to make even a wild guess at how many hours of television we watch because television has become an integral part of our lives.

Almost every child growing up in the United States today displays some symptoms of television addiction. Obviously, the heavy viewer (fifty hours or more a week) will exhibit more blatant symptoms than the child who views only fifteen hours a week. But one thing is certain: the vid-kid is everywhere.

According to a study done in Boston back in 1959, it was the blue collar worker and his family who were the most dependent on TV.[1] Among the middle class there seemed to be a taboo about too much television watching. Not so today. Every home, regardless of class, is wired to the hilt. Video centers, complete with nine-foot screens, playback units, and video discs adorn most family rooms. In the summertime upper- and middle-class families depart for the shore equipped with everything needed for survival, including the Sony portable. Families check into remote mountain retreats ostensibly to get away from it all, but almost certainly a small television is tucked in among their baggage. Recently, a young teenager we know went on a tenday ski trip with a well-educated New York family. When not on the slopes, the family spent every spare minute, including meals, watching television or arguing about what to watch. Even Dr. Spock is not immune. He took his stepdaughter and granddaughter to New York for a tour of the museums and recalled the disaster in a *Newsweek* article. "I couldn't get them away from the goddamned TV set in the hotel room. It made me sick."[2]

Who is the vid-kid? How can you recognize the symptoms? On the opposite page you'll find a checklist that highlights some key questions about your children's daily habits and gives you a quick insight into whether they're hooked on television. The rest of this chapter discusses in more detail danger signals that could indicate your children may be on the way to having serious problems, many of which will be related to television.

CHECKLIST: Do Your Children Watch Too Much Television?

1. Do your children come straight home from school and head for the TV set?
2. Do they spend Saturday morning in front of television?
3. In their spare time do they turn to television first and other activities second?
4. Do they watch television before school?
5. Do they play with toys while the television is turned on?
6. Do they play with friends in front of the television?
7. Do your children frequently say they're bored?
8. Do your children nag you for TV toys and Junk food?
9. Are the majority of the toys your children play with electronic related?
10. Are your children under 12 still awake at 10:00 P.M.?
11. Is the television on during mealtimes?
12. Is much of the mealtime conversation television-related?
13. Do your children ask to arrange meals, family activities, and life in general around what's going to be on television?

Most parents of preschool children will readily identify some of the vid-kid symptoms. Parents of older children may have to rely on their teachers for confirmation of addiction because it is in school, in the group setting, that vid-kid symptoms are most apparent.

Does Your Child Need Immediate Gratification? Does He Lack Tolerance?

We all hope to raise children who are patient, thoughtful, and kind; in short, we want our children to be well-mannered and considerate of others. Television often works against the achievement of these goals, however.

Take Jeremy, for example—a bright second-grade boy from Teaneck, New Jersey. According to his teacher, Jeremy is extremely impatient when she isn't quick to give answers to problems. "He can never wait while I help other children." A closer look at Jeremy's habits reveals that he is an avid television watcher. What's more, his parents think it's cute the way he talks back to the television, figuring out endings to programs before they have run their course. Jeremy, obviously programmed for issues to be resolved in thirty minutes or less, has little patience when problems in the real world take longer to solve.

Impatience is a major issue as soon as

children enter kindergarten. Many preschool teachers repeat time and again that five year olds want the teacher to do it all. Gone are the days when free play got children involved with their favorite fantasies and they really knew how to participate with others. Today, the attitude among kindergartners is, "Do it for me!" The teachers say they want it all done for them, step by step, laying out their programs of play.

"My class is full of Jeremies," concurs a second-grade teacher from Montclair, New Jersey. "They put their hands in the air and shout, 'Me, me, me! Call on me!' When I do, the child gives an answer and then is finished learning for the day. He doesn't care at all what any other classmate has to say. Most of my class is very self-centered."

Others hypothesize that television children have little tolerance because for the most part their lives have very little conflict or struggle. Every day is programmed. Toddlers and school children alike seem to have lives full to the brim with activities, play groups, sports, and so on. When there are time gaps, when suddenly there is nothing to do, most children and their parents count on television to fill the void. A problem arises when the daily program goes awry, and the TV child has no access to the tube. The child's flexibility comes up short, his patience is tried, and he often loses his bearings. Having strayed so far from creative play and the ability to entertain himself, this child is at a loss and has trouble functioning.

In a 1977 report on television *Newsweek* stated that elementary school teachers complain that children today are conditioned to see problems resolved quickly, frustrating them when they are faced with the longer, more involved problems that are an integral part of real learning. These children, *Newsweek* claims, are quickly turned off by any activity that promises less than instant gratification.

"Each day we cover reading, math, phonics, and spelling projects in the second grade," says teacher Mary Signer. "Many children may finish only two of the assignments and not do those very well. They just don't have the will to work at things. I work like mad, constantly trying to get their attention. Perhaps if I performed like a TV character, they would respond. But I refuse. They must learn how to deal with people."

Other teachers have succumbed to the trap. "It's really important to be an actress," says Jamie Figenbaum, a sixth-grade teacher. "Every day I go to work and plan my show. It's actually as if I'm on stage."

Television children seem to want quick solutions, tying problems up any old way and moving on to the next thing. If something doesn't work well or come easily, they just switch to the next "channel."

Does Your Child Have Behavior Problems, Such as Violent or Aggressive Play, Lack of Self-Control, or Overactivity?

Veteran teachers assert that children are in trouble today because by the time they arrive at the kindergarten door, they have learned all sorts of sounds, words, and letters but have skipped important developmental growth stages along the way. These "new children," as opposed to the "old ones" of fifteen or twenty years ago, have been grossly affected by television, and it shows in their behavior. Teachers say that most of their work with TV children consists of continually adjusting the curriculum to accommodate their overstimulated senses.

"Many children come to school revved up like the cars on 'The Dukes of Hazzard,' " reports kindergarten teacher Cathy Marino. "They career around the room, swooping over and under everything in sight, totally overstimulated from their morning dose of the tube. These children have an awfully hard time coming down to earth. They can't sit still; they can't focus or follow directions. Hyperactivity goes hand in hand with the inability to concentrate on anything for very long. And if you can't get them to focus, you can't get them to think and learn."

Sheila Jones, a first-grade teacher, sees

many cases of the hyperactive child. "One little boy I have this year can't sit," she says. "He goes to the water fountain, then to the pencil sharpener, and finally when he has no place left to go he falls backward out of his chair. This may happen three times a day. He doesn't do it for a joke. He really can't stay in a seated position."

This restless, unfocused behavior is quite a change from the old days. Twenty years ago, veteran teachers recall, block building was a big hit with little boys. They would spend hours making buildings, streets, and signs. Today, block building consists of explosions and other destruction. Twenty years ago, the housekeeping corner was for Mommy and Daddy and children. Today the corner is rarely used, but when it is, the children often pretend that the family is warding off a burglar. Sirens and arriving police complete the scene. Twenty years ago, many children had a favorite corner or a special toy at school. Today children run randomly from one thing to another, rarely spending more than a few minutes on any object.

For all of these reasons many schools have begun to make recommendations to parents concerning their chilren's TV viewing. The New Canaan Country School in Connecticut warns in a special brochure that parents must protect their children from the temptation of TV addiction. Kimberton Farms School in Pennsylvania gives written guidelines to parents concerning their children's television habits. They recommend no television for children through the first grade and no television during the week for older students. In Littleton, Colorado, the school committee distributed the "Kid-Vid Guide" advising parents how to choose programs and setting specific time limits on television viewing.

Is Your Child Sleepy, Listless, or Dazed?

It has often been noted that after watching television many children have a dull look in their eyes, as if they've been hypnotized. One simple answer is that television children have a dazed look because of their sleep patterns. As a rule, TV-addicted children get far too little sleep.

Five-year-old Scotty has older siblings who regularly watch television at night, sometimes as late as one in the morning. Therefore, Scotty also gets his share of late-night television because his family generally forgets he is in the room. One person who does notice, however, is his teacher. "Scotty arrives at school with circles under his eyes down to his cheekbones," she says. "He walks in like a zombie and is dazed for most of the morning."

When children are tired, they are unable to focus on what is being taught. "Susan is in dreamland," her teacher reports. "I

figure she watches six or more hours of
television a night—you know, all those
romantic-escape programs like 'Loveboat.'
She comes to school literally dreaming of
being somewhere else. When I call on her to
answer a question, it's rare that she can
conjure up anything to say. Usually she
stalls with 'ums' and 'likes' and finally, with
further probing, says something almost totally unrelated to the subject at hand."

The stories go on and on. "Elizabeth
yawns constantly, from the Pledge of Alle-
giance until the three o'clock bell. During
the day she almost constantly has her head
down on the desk, and she writes in a prone
position. Many TV programs she talks
about are shown at 10 p.m. Other children
in Elizabeth's class look as if they've been
drugged," reports her angry teacher.

One teacher told me that last year she
asked three different mothers to take their
children to the doctor for physicals because
she thought they were sick. "It doesn't seem
natural to me to see children all pale and
passive, not able to muster energy to do a
minimum of work."

Another answer to why television children appear so listless may lie in the fact
that too much television lulls the viewer
into a passive state. Viewer after viewer
will attest that he doesn't really watch television but passively stares at it. Peter
Crown, a physiological psychologist, likens
television to a fire. "Just as gazing into a

campfire can be absorbing and hypnotic, so can gazing at a TV screen. It doesn't matter what's on; it only matters that there is something emitting changing patterns of light to capture the attention."[3]

Marie Winn raises the question of whether excessive viewing can lead to over-development of the nonverbal, visual aspect of children's development at the expense of their ability to use words and logic. She points out that, in the adult, the cerebral cortex, the part of the brain that governs thinking, is divided into two hemispheres. The left governs most of the active verbal and logic processes and the right, though less well understood, is involved with visual and spatial relations. In young children the hemispheres of the brain do not specialize, but as children learn to speak and think, Winn assumes verbal processes play a growing role in their development. What happens if children spend their formative years watching television? "As the child takes in television words and images hour after hour, day after day, with little of the mental effort that forming his own thoughts and feelings and molding them into words would require, as he *relaxes* year after year, a pattern emphasizing nonverbal cognition becomes established. . . . [He becomes] once again, the passive captive of his own sensation [that] he was when nonverbal thought was his only means of learning."[4]

Given these observations, it's hard not

to believe that excessive television may be one major reason for the listless, passive children teachers are seeing at school. And sadder still, these children are cajoled into staying tuned into passivity because television's voice constantly advises, "We'll be right back," "Stay right where you are," and "Don't miss the upcoming special this Friday night." So the children sit still, just as they are told, going into an ever-deepening video trance.

Does Your Child Avoid Tasks and Block Out Responsibilities? Does He Have Trouble Relating to People?

The television children of today listen much less carefully than in years past, teachers report. Important listening skills are all but dead.

"Drew hates math," confides his teacher. "The minute I say, 'Take out your math books,' he flicks off the channel, which is me, and withdraws into himself. He's not the only one. Many of my children are very adept at tuning out whatever they choose *not* to deal with."

Margaret Giro, a third-grade teacher from New Jersey, theorizes, "Today's child, from infancy, has been surrounded by noise from television, the stereo, and the radio. For simple survival from so much stimulation, little children instinctively learn to shut out the background noise. By the time they come to school they have adopted a very sophisticated skill of blocking out school background noise. I think, after a while, the teacher's voice also becomes background noise. They simply tune me out when they're sick of listening."

Writer and critic Clifton Fadiman talks of television land as the "alternate life." He explains what teachers such as Mrs. Giro are working against.

> *Good teachers almost always admit that their difficulties stem from competition with the "alternate life." And this competition they are not trained to meet. The "alternate life" has one special psychological effect that handicaps the teacher. The effect is the decline in the faculty of attention and, therefore, a decline in the capacity to learn—not an innate capacity, but the capacity as it is conditioned by the media. The great attraction of the media is that they do the mental work for you and when they do exact attention, it is only for a brief period of time.[5]*

The results of such avoidance can be disastrous for learning. Children who tune out are simply refusing to interact, and without interaction there can be no learning. By watching television, day in and day out, children eventually become spectators rather than participants in life.

The ability to relate to people is the next casualty of television-watching children. Evenings used to be the time for family conversations and family activities. Parenting by machine has replaced much of the human interaction, as well as after school smalltalk. Dr. David Pearl, a researcher at the National Institute of Mental Health, suspects that "television has displaced much of the normal interaction between parents and children, those kinds of interactions that are essential for maximum development."[6]

Most disconcerting is an American Academy of Pediatrics statement that suggests a remarkable likeness between the classic posture of a drug addict and that of a child TV viewer. "Both actions serve to remove the child from his environment, to blot out the real world," says Edward Kittrell, chief of the Department of Communications for the academy.[7] Similarly, *War on Drugs Magazine* is beginning to run articles linking television to the drug culture. Marie Winn and other experts have made connections between television addiction and the increased use of real drugs.

Day-to-day contact with people is crucial to sound child development. Psychologist Bruno Bettelheim, who is deeply concerned with television's effect on social relations, says, "Children who have been taught, or conditioned, to listen passively most of the day to the warm verbal communications

coming from the TV screen, to the deep emotional appeal of so-called TV personalities,
are often unable to respond to real persons
because they arouse so much less feeling
than the skilled actor. Worse, they lose the
ability to learn from reality because life
experiences are much more complicated than
the ones they see on the screen."[8]

Is Your Child Very Fearful?
Does He Have Nightmares?

"I didn't have to hold on to my teddy
bear quite so hard last week," recalled
Johnny Donovan after participating in a
No-TV Week at his school. "When I stopped
watching television, I stopped getting scared
at night." It had been just a week before
that many of Johnny's classmates had been
permitted to watch a made-for-TV-movie
about a baby alligator that grew to mon-
strous proportions in a city's water system.
The day after the movie, Johnny and his
friends were overcome with fear. "I was
afraid to go to the bathroom in the middle
of the night because the alligator might be
in my toilet," whispered a little girl. Others
weren't going to take baths until they were
sure the alligator had moved on to another
town.

"Parents just don't seem to realize that
the last thing children see or hear before
bedtime is what stays in their subconscious

and becomes part of the sleep experience," says kindergarten teacher Cathy Marino. "The children believe what they see, particularly if they are watching alone in a darkened room and have no one to talk to about what's up there on the screen."

For generations of children, the bedtime ritual has been a story while cuddling with parents, prayers, a hug, and a kiss. Today, however, many children go to sleep with only the television playing in the background. According to my informal polls with families and schoolchildren, many children have television sets in their rooms, and the set serves as a real companion morning, noon, and night.

Third grader Ellen Goodman confesses that because she has a television in her room, and because it lulls her to sleep, she frequently experiences nightmares. "There's always some show that scares me," she says. When asked why she just doesn't turn the television off at bedtime, she responds with fervor, "Oh, that would be even worse. I would feel so alone!"

Thirty years ago, a study in which teachers interviewed two thousand six year olds in private and parochial schools found that more than half the children dreamed about the television programs they watched, and almost all of those interviewed said that their resultant dreams were bad.[9] If this was the case back in the fifties, when television was a mildly tame medium, consider what the results of a similar study would be today.

A survey designed by the Foundation for Child Development and conducted by Temple University in 1977 revealed that heavy TV viewers (in this case children between seven and eleven years old) were likely to be scared often, fearful of the world at large, frightened that someone bad will come into their house, and afraid that when they go outside someone will hurt them.[10]

Because of the graphic nature of television and its ability to bring horror and brutality into the "safe" haven of the home, teachers report a rise in the fear quotient of students, as well as a preoccupation with monsters, aliens, and other such video characters. One second-grade teacher reports that an exceptionally heavy TV viewer in her class is so preoccupied with monsters that most of his compositions include these characters. "Even when the assigned subject has nothing to do with these creatures," reports the teacher, "he manages to weave these monsters into his work."

Just as there appears to be a link between viewing violence on television and violent behavior, so there appears to be a link between seeing scary programs and frightened children. The problem is that most children see a great deal of adult programming which not only frightens them but also portrays the world as a place full of people bent on committing crimes—a far cry from the world most children will grow up to live in.

Does Your Child Have Trouble Expressing Himself? Does Your Child Talk TV Talk?

We once lived next door to a boy named Bobby, who was smart as a whip but terribly uncoordinated. His speech was usually unintelligible and nasal, and he had a lisp. At the time we didn't think much about it. We did know, however, that Bobby's mother had a low threshold for noise, and at the slightest commotion Bobby and his brother would be sent off to their rooms, where Bobby and his television would commiserate. It took diagnosis by a speech pathologist to recognize that Bobby had had very little practicing speaking, and had learned his speech patterns from television. To improve his language ability, Bobby had to be taken off television completely.

This is not an extreme case. There have been many research studies on this subject, and teachers concur that hours spent in one-way communication can lead to any one of a myriad of speech problems. At the least it can place young children on the wrong track.

"What you talkin' about, man?" shouts five-year-old Craig as he jumps to his feet, hands on hips in imitation of Arnold on "Different Strokes," and demands an explanation of a lesson. Craig has Arnold down pat, and it doesn't matter that his teacher is a woman, not a man. After such an explosion, and his teacher reports there are several a day, the class breaks up.

One teacher interviewed believed it was necessary for preschoolers to develop vocabulary and language skills so they will be ready to move on to the more difficult skill of reading. "Television takes them off the track of what we are trying to do, and so the greater part of the day is used up redirecting thinking and language learned from television toward the task at hand."

"The only way language is developed," says Cathy Marino, "is by getting them talking to other people. It's give and take. I can just about tell by the end of the first week of school who's addicted to television by listening to speech patterns and sentence structure."

Some experts say many television children are likely to have a richer vocabulary but only superficial comprehension of what words mean. However, Mary Signer, a teacher of twenty years' classroom experience, disagrees. "I've found that each year their vocabularies diminish. I was stunned to find out that my second-graders didn't know the meaning of the words 'silo' or 'crane.' There is only so much teaching that can go on in school. After hours children need books read to them, exposure to new environments, and things pointed out and explained to them."

Television teenagers are a perfect example of people unable to express themselves. Even the verbal scores on Scholastic Aptitude Testing (SAT) examinations have steadily declined 200 points since 1964, when the first television-generation class graduated from high school. After years of living with and studying to television programs, television children end up with incomplete thought patterns and video vocabularies. This takes us back to the University of Toronto study that compared the language of children's books, which not only offered a wide and varied vocabulary but increasingly complicated sentence structures, with the limited vocabulary and sentence structure used on television. You only have to talk with the average teenager to realize that television has arrested his capacity to deliver full-blown verbal thought. "The dominant means of communication in our society—words—does not seem adequate for people of the new consciousness," wrote Charles Reich of the people who grew up on television.[11]

The last time I tried to talk to a group of teenagers, I counted thirty-two "likes," innumerable "um's," and several "wow's" and "maybe's." Putting aside the teenager's natural desire not to talk with adults, it seems that teenagers today hesitate inordinately, as if speaking were actually painful. Teachers of teens say their students stall, as if waiting for words to come out, but lack the capacity to force them to the surface. The television child will never be articulate unless he begins to ask more questions, exercise his brain, expand his thoughts.

Does Your Child Ask for Toys and Foods Advertised on Television?

One of the most unpleasant sights in contemporary life can be seen almost daily in any supermarket. A mother is pushing a shopping cart with one child sitting in front and another tagging along behind, when all of a sudden both children spot the Sugar Smacks or the Hawaiian Punch or whatever else is currently being advertised on children's TV programs. The children start in with minor requests; "Please can we buy it? Why can't we buy it?" The mother counters with, "No, we don't need it, besides, it has too much sugar. It isn't good for you." To which the children reply with more nagging or maybe tears and tantrums. The mother is left with almost no choice. She either puts the product into the cart or says a firm "no" and faces miserable children for the rest of her shopping session. This country is loaded with miniconsumers who are ready to buy whatever is being sold on television.

"You should see the children's letters to Santa Claus," says a second-grade teacher. "Last year I had them write not only what they wanted to receive but also a little story about how good they had been, how they had helped their mother, and so on. When a newspaper reporter came to class to cover the story, he was astounded at what he found. There were letters all right, but they only contained long, long lists of things the children wanted, all copied right from television commercials." Yesterday's child found it easy to ask Santa for as many things as could be thought of, but today's television child rattles off a super-long list of objects that couldn't possibly have been known about unless he literally lived in the toy store. Television has practically brought the store into the home.

According to Television Awareness Training, a group dedicated to helping the public become critical viewers, most of today's toys are designed with one major consideration. Will the toy make a good TV commercial? It's important for us to realize that television is a means of selling things. There is entertainment and information, but in order to put a program on the air, it needs a sponsor. According to F. Earle Barcus, professor of communications at Boston University, "TV ads probably have more effect on children than any other form of programming. Everyone has had the experience of seeing a two-year-old playing on the floor, and when the commercial comes on, he stops to watch it."[12]

When a company is spending more than $100,000 a minute, you can be sure it tries hard to reach its designated audience. Over $600 million dollars is spent annually on advertising pitched to children.[13] Further, more than 70 percent of the ads on Saturday morning television sell sugar-coated products, hooking children on bad eating habits before they can develop defenses against such products.

Many toys advertised on television are battery operated, leaving little to the imagination; push a button and it goes. Eventually, with uncreative toys you will have less creative children. "The vid-kid toys come with built-in fantasies," says University of Virginia psychology professor Stephen Worchel. "The children's playground activities have been programmed by last night's shows. You don't see kids making their own toys out of crummy things the way we used to."[14]

Consumer advocate Robert Choate was so incensed by the commercialization of the nation's young that he took his case to Senate hearings. "In the 1930s a mother fended off aggressive door-to-door salesmen eager to get Junior's ear. Today she is told to protect the innocent while twenty-two salespeople per hour beseech her child over the tube, disguised as the friendly folk of cartoon jingle or adventureland."[15]

Is Your Child Constantly Bored and Unable to Amuse Himself?

Perhaps the most devastating consequence to the television generation is the sad fact that today's child is growing up bored and unable to amuse himself. Ten or fifteen years ago children still knew how to play. Games of hopscotch, jump rope, jacks, and other street sports were common sights, but television has helped to make outdoor play a thing of the past. Most working mothers feel secure only if they know where their children are after school, and that often means sitting motionless in front of television. Children's curiosity and interest in toys and games have died, and we are seeing a generation of children who have forgotten how to amuse themselves unless a program of play or work is provided by a parent or teacher.

"It's apparent to me," says a fourth-grade teacher, "that children don't have the inclination to amuse themselves. My room is chock-full of beautiful books, math games, story starters, and film loops, but when the children finish an assignment and have some spare time, it's rare that they gravitate to other projects. I must always give them a specific task. The same is true on the play-ground. More often than not they stand around wondering what they can do when right in front of them are monkey bars, swings, and balls."

"I have great distress when I give children an assignment to draw a picture of what they did the day before. Do you know how many blank pieces of paper I see?" asks a second-grade teacher. "Some of their minds are so muddled with television images and so lacking in imaginative powers that they can't recall what happened yesterday."

"Everything's boring," says a sixth-grade teacher. "That is definitely the key word, and I hear it a hundred times a day."

How do teachers respond? One admits to being angry about having to resort to gimmicky minishows, lots of visuals, and daily events just to keep children from boredom. Cathy Marino was embarrassed to admit that she went so far as to design a cardboard television box behind which she stages puppet shows. "I even get behind the box occasionally and put on a show."

The most addicted TV children are known to throw up their hands and burst into tears if a teacher's request seems too complicated. The surface excuse is boredom; on closer inspection, however, the step-by-step process of tedious schoolwork is far too exhausting and involved for a child who does not know how to amuse himself. Educators agree that television children simply don't want to have to do something for themselves. They want it done for them.

In one of her papers, Dr. Dorothy Cohen told of a five year old who said to his teacher: "I like to turn things on and watch it. I don't want to make anything." Dr. Cohen questions this attitude: "Is this what happens when too many of children's experiences in life are with images instead of real things, with cartoons instead of real people, are passive instead of active? Where is the child who wanted to do nothing but play? Who built sand castles and bridges and houses? Who skipped and hugged and fought?"[16]

I'm afraid the answer to her question is simple. Today's child is home in his electronic house, bored to pieces, with the television.

Is Your Child Having Trouble with Schoolwork?

Ultimately, all of the previous symptoms come to bear on a child's ability to learn, to assimilate information and to digest intellectual material. Too much television works against the techniques for learning used in most schools.

Major studies concerning television's effects are finally proving what many critics of the medium have long been suggesting. Television has affected the ability to learn. One of the most comprehensive studies was completed last year by the California Department of Education, which surveyed 520,000 students in the sixth and twelfth grades. "There is an absolute drop in scores as you watch more TV," says Alex Law, head of program and evaluation for the

California schools. "Your brightest kids are just as affected and in some cases more so than average kids. . . . All you have to do is listen to a sitcom to realize that students who spend six hours a night with this kind of programming aren't going to develop high-level skills."[17] Further, students who read more score higher on achievement tests, perhaps because when they're reading they obviously aren't watching television.

Researcher Michael Morgan at the Annenberg School of Communications also believes that the medium is powerful enough to override other factors. "Heavy viewing may do the most damage among kids who would most likely be higher achievers," he says. "Even when youngsters had higher I.Q.'s and higher aspirations, which would usually lead to higher achievement, their test scores were as low as those of students from more modest backgrounds if they watched a lot of TV."[18]

Researchers can't point to the reasons for the relationship between television viewing and lower achievement, although some believe it is the poor quality of the content and the dialogue. Nor can television be blamed for all school problems. Its pervasiveness suggests, however, that it plays a major role. It is one of the few experiences that all Americans share; as we have seen, it is in almost every home, and viewing is the number-one recreational activity in the country. At the same time elementary school teachers are reporting students unable or unwilling to learn, a blue-ribbon panel named by the College Entrance Examination Board labeled television as one of the reasons for the decline in SAT scores, and colleges are offering courses in remedial reading and writing. The novelist Jerzy Kosinski said in an interview that the effects of television could be readily observed: "Go into any high school and see how limited the students' perception of themselves is, how crippled their imagination, how unable to tell a story, to read and concentrate, or even to describe an event accurately a moment after it happens. See how easily they are bored, how quickly they take up the familiar reclining position in the classroom, how short their attention span is."[19]

These are the students who learned to "read" TV-style, via "Sesame Street," who cannot sustain interest in an image for more than eight seconds, according to producers of film strips for high schools. "The electronic medium, with its emphasis on visual imagery, immediacy, nonlinearity, and fragmentation, does not give support to attitudes that are fundamental to the classroom," says Professor Postman.[20]

If your child is having school problems, they may be easily corrected by a simple flick of the switch to OFF.

Notes

1. Kent Geiger and Robert Sokol, "Social Norms in Television Watching," *American Journal of Sociology*, 1959, 174–181.

2. Quoted by Harry Waters, "What TV Does to Kids," *Newsweek*, February 21, 1977, p. 63.

3. Quoted by Barry Siegel, "Is Television a Medium That Muddles the Mind?" *St. Petersburg Times*, March 12, 1979.

4. Marie Winn, *The Plug-In Drug*, Bantam, 1978, pp. 42–53.

5. "Classroom's Ubiquitous Rival: Pop Culture," *New York Times*, June 13, 1979.

6. Quoted by James Monaco, *Media Culture*, Delta, 1978, p. 250.

7. Quoted by Mariani, "The Impact of TV Violence on Your Children," *Family Weekly*, November 11, 1979, p. 32.

8. *The Informed Heart*, Free Press, 1960, p. 50.

9. Hal Evry, "TV Murder Caused Bad Dreams," *Film World*, August 1952, p. 247.

10. Cited in Richard Flaste, "Survey Finds That Most Children Are Happy at Home But Fear World," *New York Times*, March 2, 1977.

11. *The Greening of America*, Random House, 1970, p. 261.

12. Quoted by Monaco *Media Culture*, p. 255.

13. Baltimore Media Alliance, P.O. Box 16262,
     Baltimore, Maryland 21210.

14. Quoted by Waters, "What TV Does to Kids."

15. Quoted by Kenneth Keniston, *All Our Chil-
     dren,* Harcourt Brace Jovanovich, 1977, p. 53.

16. "Is TV a Pied Piper?" *Young Children
     Journal,* November 1974, p. 12.

17. Cited in "Schoolwork Undermined by TV,
     California Survey Shows," *Report on Edu-
     cational Research,* November 26, 1980, pp.
     1–2.

18. Quoted by Gene Maeroff, "Specific TV Shows
     Tied to Child's Achievement," *New York
     Times,* March 30, 1982.

19. "Television and Values," The Learning Seed
     Company, June 24, 1979, p. 15.

20. "Order in the Classroom," *Atlantic Monthly,*
     September 1979, p. 35.

5
THE FOUR-WEEK NO-TV PROGRAM

Y ou've come far enough in this book now to know that television can affect many aspects of family life and child development and are probably wondering just how firmly rooted television is in your household.

Abuse of television is just like being overweight or smoking too much. You're not going to go on a rigorous diet unless you truly feel unhappy with your flabby stomach, tight waistband, or popped buttons. It's the same with smoking. When it affects your health, when you find yourself huffing and puffing after a simple walk up a flight of stairs or gasping for breath on the tennis court, then and only then will the average person take up a plan of action to stop smoking.

So it is with overuse of television.

Are your children staring at the box when you really wish they were outside playing? Is your day organized around a soap-opera schedule? Are you increasingly aware of the buzz of television sets coming out of each bedroom every evening? Then it's time for your family to take the following TV Quiz and see where you stand. Have each family member fill in his or her own test.

The TV Quiz

1. How many television sets do you own?
   1 2 3 4 5 6 7   _____/_____

2. How many are color sets?
   1 2 3 4   _____/_____

3. How many are black-and-white sets?
   1 2 3 4   ____0____

4. Where are the sets located?
   Living Room, Bedroom, Kitchen
   Family Room   ___LR___

5. How many hours a day do you watch TV?
   1 2 3 4 5 6 7 8   ____3____

6. How many hours of TV does each
   child watch?
   1 2 3 4 5 6 7 8   ____4____

7. Do you watch TV alone or with others?
   Alone, with others, both   ____b____

8. Do you watch TV because you are bored
   or have nothing else to do?
   Yes, no   ____y____

9. Do you turn off a show that doesn't
   interest you?
   Yes, no, sometimes   ____s____

10. Does your set(s) remain on for long
    periods of time even when you or your

family is not watching it/them?
Yes, no, sometimes   *No*

11.   Do you watch TV in bed at night?
      Yes, no, sometimes   *No*

12.   Is TV on during mealtimes?
      Yes, no, sometimes   *S*

13.   Do you turn your set off when
      someone drops in?
      Yes, no   *No*

14.   Do certain shows affect you
      emotionally?
      Yes, no, sometimes   *Y*

15.   Do you turn on the set to entertain
      your preschool children?
      Yes, no, sometimes   *No*

16.   Do you watch TV mainly to relax?
      Yes, no   *Y*

17.   Would you miss TV if you didn't
      have a set?
      Yes, no   *No*

How to Score Your TV Watching

1.   5 points for each set
2.   5 points for each set
3.   2 points for each set
4.   5 points each
5.   1 point for each hour
6.   1 point for each hour for each child
7.   Alone (5)   others (2)   both (3)
8.   Yes (5)   no (2)
9.   Yes (0)   no (5)   sometimes (3)
10. Yes (5)   no (0)   sometimes (3)
11. Yes (5)   no (0)   sometimes (3)
12. Yes (5)   no (0)   sometimes (3)
13. Yes (0)   no (5)
14. Yes (5)   no (2)   sometimes (3)
15. Yes (5)   no (0)   sometimes (3)
16. Yes (5)   no (2)
17. Yes (5)   no (0)

How to Interpret the Quiz

A score of 90 or above signifies that television has invaded your life and you should try to get your habit under control. If you scored from 75 to 90, you are a borderline TV addict and should take some steps to cut down on your viewing. Under 70 points means you have a television conscience and probably don't need any help controlling your television viewing.

Don't be surprised if you scored over 85. Ninety percent of the people who have taken this test score well over 85, and there is no reason you should be different. After all, television was designed to entice, entertain, electrify, and hold its viewers, so it's not your fault that it has wormed its way into your home. It's also not your fault that you have fallen into the trap of parenting by machine, using TV as a babysitter.

However, after reading the symptoms and dangers of television addiction, it is your fault if you allow yourself and your family to continue to be held by television. It's time to break your TV habit and begin to control your television viewing rather than the other way around.

With your newly developed consciousness, you know now what must be done— turn off the television and turn on your brain. It's time to speak up to yourself and, more importantly, speak back to the television. In short, you are on the brink of getting unplugged. How do you start?

The Four-Week No-TV Program I am about to describe has been adapted from the No-TV Week programs I have conducted in elementary schools and parent workshops. You and your family can try the program alone, or you can interest a group in undertaking the program with you. There are arguments for both approaches. On the one hand, it's fun to embark on an adventure alone; on the other, in the case of cutting the TV cord, some people (especially children) find it easier to succeed if they are working at withdrawal with friends. Whether you decide to go it alone or work together with church members, a school group, or neighbors, you yourself must be convinced of the value of controlling TV watching and you must be firmly set on a clear course. To keep your purpose in mind, post this list prominently in your home, so you can turn to it whenever you feel yourself wavering.

The Four-Week No-TV Program is a process of gradual withdrawal from television designed to make all family members —adults and children alike—aware of themselves in relation to television and to help each person see the opportunities for enrichment and the exciting activities that are available when television is no longer constantly there.

Six Reasons to Break the TV Habit

1. Children must learn to live their own lives before they learn TV lives.
2. It is imperative for an *individual* child to emerge in the early years, not a pretaped version.
3. It is not in a child's nature to be unhappy. A child may be bored temporarily without TV, but he will soon devise a path of happy, active living.
4. We must not lose the art of childhood. This culture needs active, imaginative children to keep fantasy and play alive.
5. Why supply children with a pseudo-life experience when their natural instinct is to do, to live?
6. Children want to relate to people rather than machines.

Week One— Watching Yourself Watching

You begin the Four-Week No-TV Program right in front of your television set. During this first week your only task will be simply to keep track of your normal daily schedule. At the end of each day, fill in the Daily Time Chart (see page 88), recording all daily activities. Make extra blank copies for all family members. Go about the business of the day including as much television as you usually watch. Then, at the end of the week, total the number of hours spent watching television for the entire week.

Encourage each member of the family to keep his or her own chart. If your children are too young to fill out their charts, have someone else do it for them. This process will be a real eye-opener, particularly for mothers, because most mothers have no idea how many hours of television their children manage to clock in one day.

All family members should participate. Your household will have an "experiment-like" attitude, which in turn will help launch your anti-TV campaign in an upbeat, cooperative atmosphere. Most families are utterly amazed at their television consumption. The children will get a kick out of checking Mom and Dad's time charts to see if the adults in the household are more addicted than they are.

While watching your favorite television shows, count the commercials in any one given hour. Be aware of the violent acts in each show, and total them up as well. Finally, make a list of some of the products advertised on TV, and then look around your house (medicine cabinet, kitchen closets) to see how much television has affected your family as consumers.

In preparation for the rest of the program, ask your children's school for any material it might have from Public Broadcasting Service on critical viewing skills.

Daily Time Chart

	Sun.	Mon.	Tues.	
6 A.M.				
7 A.M.				
8 A.M.				
9 A.M.				
10 A.M.				
11 A.M.				
12 noon				
1 P.M.				
2 P.M.				
3 P.M.				
4 P.M.				
5 P.M.				
6 P.M.				
7 P.M.				
8 P.M.				
9 P.M.				
10 P.M.				
11 P.M.				
Total TV Hours				

TOTAL HOURS OF TV WATCHED THIS WEEK:

Wed.	Thurs.	Fri.	Sat.

Recommended books for your children are Roald Dahl's *Charlie and the Chocolate Factory* (Knopf, 1964; Bantam, 1979) and Terry W. Phelan's *The Week Mom Unplugged the TVs* (Four Winds, 1979). Your local librarian will be able to direct you to the American Library Association's annual compilation of Notable Books, grouped by age for children, and of Best Books for Young Adults; the ALA also has a list of all the picture and storybooks that have won the association's major prizes. Other helpful guides on books to read during the Four-Week No-TV Program are available from the Children's Book Council (67 Irving Place, New York, New York 10003), which publishes a booklet called "Children's Choices," grouped by age, every year.

Week Two—Take a Critical Look

Continue television watching during Week Two, but start viewing with a more critical eye. At the beginning of each day decide precisely *which* programs you intend to watch and *why* you plan to watch them.

After watching each program, rate the show excellent, good, fair, or poor.
Factors to be taken into consideration during this rating game are:
• *Quality of the script:* Is the situation realistic? Are the jokes

funny? Do the characters act like real people? Is the dialogue of high quality?

• *Extent of violence:* Was the violence on the program necessary? Did it scare you? Was it appropriate for children's viewing?

• *Degree of honesty:* Did the story really answer the questions it raised? In the case of a documentary, was the subject dealt with comprehensively?

• *Entertainment:* Was the program worth the time you spent watching it? Did you feel happy and uplifted after watching? Was it a good escape?

Use the accompanying Program Chart to assist you with your new critical approach to television. Children may need some help filling in their charts. You may consider setting aside an hour during the evening when, as a family, you fill in your charts. Discuss each person's rating of specific shows.

At the end of Week Two ask yourself the following questions.

How many shows did I watch this week? Did I watch more or less than usual? If I decided not to watch TV at a given time, what did I replace it with?

Program Chart

Choose from the following for your reason for watching a particular show: Entertainment, Pleasure, Relaxation, Nothing Else to Do, Information, Other. Choose from the following for your rating of each show: Excellent, Good, Mediocre, Bad.

Sun.	Program to Watch: Reason: Rating: Instead of watching I decided to:	Program to Watch: Reason: Rating: Instead of watching I decided to:
Mon.	Program to Watch: Reason: Rating: Instead of watching I decided to:	Program to Watch: Reason: Rating: Instead of watching I decided to:
Tues.	Program to Watch: Reason: Rating: Instead of watching I decided to:	Program to Watch: Reason: Rating: Instead of watching I decided to:

Program to Watch:	Program to Watch:
Reason:	Reason:
Rating:	Rating:
Instead of watching I decided to:	Instead of watching I decided to:
Program to Watch:	Program to Watch:
Reason:	Reason:
Rating:	Rating:
Instead of watching I decided to:	Instead of watching I decided to:
Program to Watch:	Program to Watch:
Reason:	Reason:
Rating:	Rating:
Instead of watching I decided to:	Instead of watching I decided to:

Wed.	Program to Watch: Reason: Rating: Instead of watching I decided to:	Program to Watch: Reason: Rating: Instead of watching I decided to:
Thurs.	Program to Watch: Reason: Rating: Instead of watching I decided to:	Program to Watch: Reason: Rating: Instead of watching I decided to:
Fri.	Program to Watch: Reason: Rating: Instead of watching I decided to:	Program to Watch: Reason: Rating: Instead of watching I decided to:
Sat.	Program to Watch: Reason: Rating: Instead of watching I decided to:	Program to Watch: Reason: Rating: Instead of watching I decided to:

Program to Watch:	Program to Watch:
Reason:	Reason:
Rating:	Rating:
Instead of watching I decided to:	Instead of watching I decided to:
Program to Watch:	Program to Watch:
Reason:	Reason:
Rating:	Rating:
Instead of watching I decided to:	Instead of watching I decided to:
Program to Watch:	Program to Watch:
Reason:	Reason:
Rating:	Rating:
Instead of watching I decided to:	Instead of watching I decided to:
Program to Watch:	Program to Watch:
Reason:	Reason:
Rating:	Rating:
Instead of watching I decided to:	Instead of watching I decided to:

What other activities did I include in the week for entertainment, relaxation, information, or companionship?

Watching critically during Week Two should point out how many of the television programs you regularly watch don't measure up to your new-found standards of good entertainment.

Week Three—Start to Cut Back

During Week Three begin, in little ways, to cut down on the entire family's TV time by following these simple rules:

1. Keep only one television in the household active. Cover any remaining sets with sheets, or store them away.
2. Eliminate TV watching before school and during meals.
3. Choose three school nights on which television cannot be watched.
4. Permit one hour of viewing on the remaining two school nights. If one hour of television is not enough for your family, then select one more hour from PBS only.
5. Determine, by family vote, how many viewing hours are to be permitted on Saturday and Sunday.
6. On Sunday look at the television section in the newspaper, and choose, as a family, the programs you will

watch each day. If family members have different interests, they may watch different programs.

7. Where appropriate, choose a family show, and watch it during your allotted time together.

Have each member fill out a copy of the accompanying Week Three TV Schedule at the beginning of the week. As a family, look at the schedules each day to see how everyone is doing and to offer encouragement.

While viewing during Week Three follow this advice from National Educational Television on good TV-viewing habits.

- Preparation is essential before watching a TV program. Know as much as possible about the program you intend to watch before it comes on. Talk about the upcoming show, and give your children something specific to look for. This will make viewing active rather than passive.
- Sitting at a direct angle and a decent distance from the set is important for good vision. Try to be ten feet away. Being too close to a color set may be a health hazard.
- Give children a goal while watching television. For example, have them listen for names and dates, differ-

Week Three TV Schedule

	Programs I Plan to Watch
Sun.	
Mon.	
Tues.	
Wed.	
Thurs.	
Fri.	
Sat.	
TOTALS	

☐ I made my week's goal.
☐ I bettered my week's goal by _____ hour(s) and _____ minutes.
☐ I didn't make my goal, but I went over by only _____ hour(s) and _____ minutes.

Name _____

	No. of Hrs. I Plan to Watch	No. of Hrs. Actually Watched	No. of Hrs. + or − Today's Goal

ences and similarities between characters, and for character motivations. With a goal in mind, attention will be heightened, and retention will be more comprehensive.

· Watch television programs with your children. Feel free to point out and talk about incidents as they happen. Make the experience a sharing one rather than an independent venture.

· When the program is over, related activities can follow: role playing, dinner table conversation, books on the program's subject matter, and so on.

Week Four—The Beginning of Life Without Television

During Week Four you will turn off your television and keep it off. Before doing this, however, sit down with your family and answer the following questions honestly:

Are we now ready to replace most of the programs watched last week with other activities?
Have we raised our levels of consciousness about television sufficiently so that we feel ready to watch less TV?

If you answered "yes" to these questions, then proceed with the program.

First, unplug all televisions, and store them away in closets or attics. Better yet, give your TVs away. At the very least you'll gain a tax deduction.

Second, don't buy *TV Guide*, and remove the TV program page from the newspaper as soon as you open it. There's no point in teasing yourself about programs you are missing.

Third, if you are addicted to a soap opera or a series, make sure you are out of the house, doing something productive and stimulating, during the time the program is on. At the very least, call a friend and have a good chat.

To help you fill in what will at first seem like long, empty hours, try some of these strategies that have been developed by schools participating in No-TV Week programs:

Record your day-to-day activities in a log, listing chores, telephone calls, radio time, time spent with friends, and so on.

Compile a list of activities to turn to in place of television.

Socialize more, and encourage your children to invite friends over.

Make this experiment a game. Design a No-TV Week button and/or signs, and display them prominently in your home. Place a sign on your unplugged

TV saying "No-TV, Please" or mark
an X in masking tape across the
screen.
Keep a diary of your feelings. This will
be a catharsis of sorts and will give
you something to turn to if withdrawal pains get severe.

The good news to remember during
Week Four is that many families have gone
before you in breaking the TV habit. They
report that the children were relieved when
the television finally went off. They enjoyed
being a family again. All families found a
new joy in recapturing time for each other
and for themselves.

Usually, the only unhappy souls at the
end of Week Four are those people who were
most addicted in the first place. Families
that house four or more televisions, video
games, and computers, who have already
given themselves over to a total electronic
hook-up will still feel some stress during
Week Four.

Initially, parents are fearful that their
role without television will become one of
magician, entertainer, and teacher all rolled
into one. However, you'll soon see that you're
no more than a catalyst. You're needed as a
facilitator or "suggestion machine" the first
few days, but then the child in your children
will return. When you're not around to encourage or suggest projects, you'll see that
your children will find their own. I guaran-

tee they won't be sitting around the house twiddling their thumbs for long. In fact, as evidenced by my workshops, no child yet has been reported to spend more than one-half hour sitting idle and angry because of no television. Within that first half hour, he may go to the refrigerator, which is the second most instant gratification after TV, and then wander on to some other activity. Left to their own devices, children will occupy their time. During this process objects never before discovered or long since forgotten will surface. After all, isn't it a child's natural instinct to play?

Having passed those first few days without television, you'll begin to notice how calm your household has become. Your family time hasn't been controlled and locked in by television programs. You have plenty of time to be together. Playing is beneficial to adults as well as children, you know. According to Frank and Theresa Caplin, founders of Creative Playthings, "When grownups stop playing, they tend to head for escape alternatives such as alcohol, drugs, and yes, even television."

Instead of burying boredom and bad moods in front of the television set, you'll find yourself talking to your children about why they sometimes feel sad, miserable, angry, and restless. Working out these feelings together is a real connection between generations. Helping your children deal with their frustrations actively rather than passively, helping them face and work out their problems rather than hiding them away in front of a TV, will really put them solidly on the path to growing up and learning how to deal with the world.

To equip your house to function without television, you'll have to fill in the blank areas created by removing your various sets. Here are a few suggestions for equally addictive but far more rewarding entertainment.

Create a Play Space

Need space? Be prepared to relinquish the dining room, a section of the family room, the basement, or any other area of your house or apartment that is attractive and available for children. Children need a private place that is theirs alone to carry out their experiments, games, and other secret activities free from the scrutiny of parents. Even if the spot is under a stairwell or in the corner of a busy room, your children will know it's theirs. Mothers, resign yourself to the fact that in these special play spaces anything goes—within reason. Children's corners will never be *Better Homes and Gardens* perfect.

Stock a Sports Center

A household sports center or dugout area is an important feature in a televisionless house. It can be a large empty closet, a series of boxes along the garage wall, or a specifically built open-cupboard area. The sports center should be filled with all kinds of equipment—gloves, bats, tees, jump ropes, roller skates, helmets, hats, rubber and tennis balls, basketballs, air pumps, and chalk to make obstacle courses, baselines, and hopscotch paths. Be willing to resupply lost balls and other equipment.

Supply a Craft Table

A dining-room table works best for a variety of crafts. Cover it with newspaper and a sheet of plastic. Along the wall build a simple bookcase area. Buy various-size baskets into which you can put crayons, beeswax, clay, glue, paint, brushes, scissors, pencils, magic markers, and other materials. Have paper, model kits, activity books, paper dolls, and anything else you can think of sitting in full view of your children. You will be amazed at how often your children will gravitate to this craft area throughout the day. A craft table is infinitely more inviting than a television screen.

During Week Four designate one or two nights for family games and projects. A family night is great for holiday projects, crafts, long games of Monopoly, or card games. Here are other family strategies and suggestions for getting through Week Four.

Resurrect the family radios and point toward one if Dad is hungry for his regular TV news.

Make sure you have activities such as crossword puzzles, needlepoint, books, and magazines readily available. Have a card table permanently set up so it is as easy to get going on a board game or a card game as it was to flip on the television.

Plan to do some major overhaul on the house such as cleaning the basement, painting the living room, or washing the windows.

Plan different menus and try new recipes. Buy a cookbook for your children so they can enjoy the art of baking. Pop popcorn. It's irresistible.

If you have a regular sporting activity, such as tennis, paddle ball, squash, or handball, arrange for additional court time, especially during your previous prime TV viewing hours.

Fix the broken bike or some other item that has been waiting to be fixed.

Plan a garage sale featuring all the items you bought because of television commercials.

Get out of the house. Go to the movies, take a walk, go out to dinner.

Renew your old hobbies. Did you have a stamp collection when you were young?

Invite another family over for dinner, potluck style, once a week.

Read your children to sleep. If they're too old for this, try reading a good short story out loud to the whole family.

Plan a family night at the library.

Sort your slides, and start up slide shows once again.

Make a scrapbook, organizing all your family pictures.

This is just the beginning of a long list of alternatives that become possible when you get television out of your life. By the time the week is over everyone will have so many projects under way and so many satisfying hours spent together as a family that you'll all be ready to think about life with limited television viewing.

6

THE MAINTENANCE PROGRAM

You have arrived. You went through an entire week with no television. Sure it took a few tough weeks to accomplish this, but don't look back now. Instead, proceed. You've worked up a momentum that will carry you through to establishing a selective, intelligent viewing program and maintaining it permanently.

Of course, you will have doubts. One day it will rain or snow, and everyone will be out of ideas for things to do. This is the time when the children used to head for the television set. Now they look up at you and practically scream, "Well, what are we going to do?" Why, you ask yourself one more time, are you depriving your children and yourself of television? Is it worth the effort? The moment these questions pop into your mind, turn to the list you have posted and read aloud the "Six Reasons to Break the TV Habit." This should remind you why you have chosen to cut down on television. But how do you go about incorporating this decision into your life?

The easiest way to begin (as I suggested for Week Four of the No-TV program) is to get rid of the family television set or to put it away. If there isn't a TV set around or access isn't easy, the problem of control is greatly reduced; however, for most families this solution isn't practical. Furthermore, after completing the Four-Week No-TV Program, most families are pretty confident that television will never again become a prominent member of their households.

Once you have taken the first steps toward breaking the TV habit, you'll need a carefully planned program to maintain control over individual and family viewing, with rules that everyone agrees to. Television time must be planned as carefully as the week's meals and activities, and you should anticipate and prepare for the times when there is a temptation to watch television heavily. It's also important to understand how video games and computers fit into a program of limited television viewing.

Working Out a Family Program

The family should first decide how many hours of viewing will be allowed each week. Many families take as their weekly maximum ten hours. According to Dr. Kenneth Hopkins, who conducted a study for the National Institute of Education entitled, "The Impact of Leisure-Time Television on School Learning," up to ten hours a week may actually enhance a student's achievement in school slightly.[1] After ten hours, however, the student's achievement level diminishes with increased viewing.

A few specific rules help bolster your television maintenance program and lead to sound viewing. Adapt your No-TV rules from those listed below. They are similar to the rules you followed during Week Three.

Rule 1. No television before school, during meals, after school, or before homework is done.

Rule 2. No televisions in the bedrooms. If possible, keep only one set active, and put it in the least inviting room of the house. Research shows that people gravitate less to the television when it's not in a main room.

Rule 3. No television on several designated nights during the week. Better yet, don't allow any regular TV viewing during the week.

Rule 4. For every half hour of television watching, one hour must be devoted to physical exercise, reading, or playing.

Rule 5. Use the record player or radio if you need background sound.

Rule 6. Don't turn on the television at

random. Watch only those programs that have been selected for the week's viewing.

Rule 7. Don't buy or read TV-related magazines.

These rules have been designed to eliminate 85 percent of all television now being watched in most households. With a little planning—that is, methodically discussing these rules point by point with the entire family—your household will be well on the way to controlling television.

For the first four to six weeks after you've completed the Four-Week No-TV Program, family members should get together on Sunday evening to review the television schedule in the newspaper and plan the week's viewing. This is the same regimen you followed during Week Three, and you can use the TV schedule on page 98 to list family and individual choices. Of course, no one *has* to watch every program that he or she has chosen. At the end of the week total everyone's hours watched and see how each of you did. After doing this for several weeks, it probably won't be necessary to fill out the charts. In fact, you may find yourself leaving notes to remind you to watch something special.

Preschool Children

Parents should plan television viewing for preschoolers, limiting children to one hour of television a day. Keep in mind that just as books are planned for different age levels, so are television programs. There is an extremely limited selection of so-called children's programming; the most obvious examples are "Captain Kangaroo," "Sesame Street," and "Mr. Roger's Neighborhood." Choose carefully among these programs, switching from one to another unless your child has a distinct preference. Try to schedule television viewing at times when older children aren't around so there won't be conflicts with siblings who are not allowed to watch during the day, or try to schedule the preschooler's viewing for family programs like "The Muppets." Children under three probably should not watch any television regularly.

Whenever possible, you should watch television with a child who is under six or seven years old, and always when a child is seeing a program for the first time, for it may be necessary to explain something. Also, television should be a social experience.

If your children had television programs they use to watch regularly, be especially sensitive to those times of the day, and plan an alternative activity so they won't feel they are missing anything.

Babysitters

Remember to tell babysitters about the no-television regimen so that house rules aren't violated as soon as you go out. Give your sitter a schedule of activities with definite times so that there's a real program to follow. For instance, if the sitter is scheduled to arrive at 6:00 and the children have already eaten dinner, there is time for a game from 6:00 to 6:30, stories from 6:30 to 7:00, a bath and getting ready for bed from 7:00 to 7:30, and a bedtime snack around 8:00.

Many young children hate to see their parents go out for the evening, but the blow is softened if they have a sitter who makes the occasions special.

Let the sitter prepare simple snacks such as popcorn, milkshakes, or ice cream cones. If the sitter is coming during the day, leave a list of games selected from "Activities in the No-TV Home," pages 129–136.

Finally, if you are down to one portable television set, keep it in the closet when a babysitter is scheduled to come. Out of sight, out of mind. You can tell the sitter where to find it if she wants to watch after the children are asleep.

Working Parents

Working parents, particularly working mothers, often depend on television as a babysitter; however, whether your children are old enough to come home to an empty house or are cared for by a babysitter or housekeeper, they can surely occupy themselves in a safe, constructive way without watching television. "We're talking about a relatively short period of time," says Jane Sherman, the mother of four children under thirteen. "Three to five is when most children of working mothers are alone. Snacks, activities, chores, and homework eat up that two hours in no time. Television is simply not a necessity." To help remind their children of this, the Shermans placed a sign on the TV screen that says, "No TV, please." What do the children do? The Shermans live in a New York City apartment and belong to a nearby gym so that the children can play indoors during the winter. In better weather there is an organized playground near their home.

For working parents who have housekeepers, conditions of employment often include the understanding that the children are not to watch television and that the set should not be on when the children are in the house. "There are so many things to do," says an editor with a leading publishing house. "My children play cards, read, build with blocks, and play with dolls. They love playtime without the structure of school."

If a working parent has followed the Four-Week No-TV Program and established television awareness in the home, then TV will cease to be a major problem after school. Assign after-school chores, and set firm after-school rules. With your children work out a list of where they can and cannot play, as well as what they can and cannot do. "I don't want my children closeted in the house, and yet I want them safe," explains one suburban mother. "They are permitted to play anywhere on our property."

Other Support Programs

Switch

Action for Children's Television, the largest and best-known group working to improve children's television and to encourage other activities, has devised a rather clever game called Switch.[2] Teach your children the five switches ACT recommends:

Switch from buying a toy to making one. In one hour of children's television it is possible to see over ten commercials for toys. These toys are often expensive—$15 to $20, more than most families can afford to spend. Instead of buying a toy, it's fun to make a puppet, plant a seed, string some spools, design a city out of cartons.

Switch to an apple, an orange, or a carrot. Ninety-eight percent of U.S. children suffer from tooth decay. The food most likely to cause cavities is sugar. With few exceptions the only foods advertised on children's television are candies, cookies, sugared cereals, drink sweeteners, and soft drinks. Stop buying those products, and dream up your own super snacks, like popcorn, cheese fingers, nuts, orange slices, and apple wedges.

Switch to public television. There is no advertising on public television. In many areas only public television stations have quality children's programming on a regular basis. In addition, there are often good dramas, concerts, documentaries, and science programs for older children.

Switch off the TV and take a walk, read a book, visit a zoo, or go to a museum. By the time the average child graduates from high school he or she has spent 15,000 hours watching television and 11,000 hours in the classroom. Sleep is the only activity which takes more time than television viewing. With less time for television your children will have more time to explore and expand their interests and play with their friends.

Switch to doing something about children's television. Talk about television to your friends and to your local station. Analyze why commercials are effective so you can see how to weaken their power over the family.

To see whether your family could benefit from switching, try this survey to gauge how deeply television has embedded itself in your household. Everyone should go through the house, particularly the kitchen cabinets, the medicine chests, and the toy shelves, identifying products bought because they were advertised on television. Make a list, so you can see how many of these products you own. The children will find it fascinating to look through their toy collection and see just how many items were advertised on television commercials or are connected with specific television programs. They may also notice that the quality of these toys is often mediocre compared to their other possessions.

Whenever possible, reinforce your stand on limiting the influence of television on your lives by not giving in to your children's demands for products advertised on television.

What to Avoid on Television

When the television is on, parents should be aware of programs to avoid when young children are around. By following these simple guidelines, you will prevent many of television's harmful aspects from affecting your children.

Avoid just watching. Turning on the television set and simply sitting in front of it is a form of escapism.

Avoid scary programs.

Avoid violent programs with a great deal of physical action.

Avoid the news when young children are in the room. If your older children watch the news, make sure an adult is with them. A mother once told me that the news was inadvertently flicked on one night when her children were present. In the first seven minutes the family saw dead Salvadoran bodies piled high, a bus accident in which nine children were killed, and the results of a disastrous flood.

Special Events

So now you've developed a house full of television consciousness with a program to back it up, and suddenly you're faced with those once in a lifetime specials that television brings right into your living room. I'm talking about live events such as the Olympic Games, presidential conventions, and the World Series and other major sports events and made-for-television documentaries or mini-series. There's no doubt that television is at its best when it is live; live coverage of special events is one of the true benefits of television. Therefore, it's surely advisable to make some exceptions for specials and major news events such as an inauguration, the release of the U.S. hostages from Iran, or the eruption of a volcano. Keep in mind, however, that prolonged viewing can disrupt the whole family's schedule, and try not to interfere with meals or the family's daily routine.

Exciting as the Olympics or a presidential convention may be, it's not a good idea to watch these events in their entirety—especially because they always come in the same year.

Here are a few suggestions for keeping abreast of special events without becoming totally glued to the television set and seduced back into heavy television viewing.

The Olympics. Watch the opening and closing ceremonies if they interest you and the summaries of daily events. In addition, choose specific events to watch, just as if you were buying tickets for them. Take in events like track and field that your children can go out and try on their own, or tune into an unusual sport to introduce the family to it. Try to avoid so-called background pieces that are designed to keep you watching the entire spectrum of Olympics coverage, even when nothing is happening. Since it's not always possible to jump up and shut the television off between major events, keep handy something to read or some project to work on. This approach will also work for others events that continue from one day to the next.

The World Series. The temptation is to watch the World Series on television. Actually, radio coverage has always been more descriptive and enthusiastic. Listen to the games for the most part, and plan to watch only the last game or two. Try to squeeze this and other sports coverage into your weekly ten-hour allotment.

Presidential conventions. Save your energy and television viewing time for the third night of the conventions, when there is actual debate over the platform and actual balloting for the candidates. And, of course, watch the acceptance speech. Children can benefit from watching the conventions, but don't overdo it. Try to steer clear of padded background coverage.

The Super Bowl. What can you say about the Super Bowl, one of the biggest TV events of the year? The hype is often greater than the game. Nevertheless, almost everyone will want to watch, so have some friends over, and make it a social occasion. For a little penance, cut down on your viewing during the rest of the week. Try the same approach with other major sports events.

Documentary dramas and mini-series. It's quite a commitment to follow a program that runs five nights in a row. However, if one of these programs seems worthwhile to a member of the family, watch the first night, catch the summary on the third night, and tune in to the final installment. For my part, I usually find a good book on the subject as informative as the television treatment. A long series, such as those featured on PBS, or a special documentary or report can easily be worked into the week's schedule as part of your regular viewing. If the series or special is scheduled for one of your no-TV nights, adjust your schedules for those weeks.

News events. A presidential news conference or major speech is valuable for older children and can be easily fitted into the week's viewing schedule. The same would hold true for space shots, major news events, and spectacles like the wedding of Prince

Charles and Lady Diana. Include these
events in your week's schedule when you
know about them in advance. If they're un-
expected but significant, adjust your viewing plan for the week, watch the events as
a family, and discuss them afterward.

Holidays

A friend of mine and her husband trav-
eled from New York to Indiana last Thanksgiving to visit her parents. The trip was
expensive, and it meant taking a few vaca-
tion days from their jobs. Thus it was both
disappointing and exasperating to them that
the television set was on during their entire
visit. "Even when friends dropped by to see
us, the set stayed on," my friend recalled.
"It seemed that television was more important to my parents than I was."

In many homes Christmas tradition has
become television specials, instead of carols
and family gatherings. When suburban New
York school children were told that they
would participate in a No-TV Week during
December, they booed because they didn't
want to miss the Christmas television specials. In 1981 there were fifty-four so-called
Christmas specials on the three major networks during a twenty-four day period.

Here are a few suggestions to keep television under control during the holidays.

Thanksgiving. This is a day for the
whole family to be together. Save the foot-

ball games for Saturday. Spend the early part of Thursday preparing the meal and readying the house, assigning jobs to each child. Stash the television in a closet, or cover it with a tablecloth and nut bowls so no one can gather around it as the day progresses.

Christmas. Choose only the very best holiday specials, and don't watch more than one a week. Instead of TV specials substitute "family specials" such as holiday crafts, baking, and reading classic Christmas stories (perhaps a long one over several nights). Invite other families to join in, or have them over for a brunch, a luncheon, or a punchbowl party.

New Year's Day. There is a Scottish tradition that on New Year's Eve and New Year's Day friends and relatives drop in on one another. Freed from television, start off the New Year with some visits or throw a big open house. Use the covered television as a buffet table.

Video Games and Computers

If you're cutting down on television viewing, where do video games and computers fit into the picture? "The trend toward electronic games and motorized, computerized robot-like toys suggests a danger that even more of our children's and our own capacities for imposing and practicing private imagery will be preempted," say

Jerome and Dorothy Singer of Yale's Television Research Center.[3] A look at the current crop of electronic devices lends credence to this statement.

Video Games

It seems apparent, at least to me, that video games, both the hand-held and arcade variety, would never have taken off in such a phenomenal way if they had not been tailor-made for the children of television. Children gravitate to video machines if for no other reason than familiarity. Video games are simply a spin-off of television, and children feel comfortable with them because they are again dealing with screens.

Several single parents I know are thrilled that their children now have something to interact with when they come home to an empty house after school. "These machines are far more imaginative than television," says one excited father. But a video machine, like television, is an isolating experience. A visit to any video arcade confirms this. The lights are dim, no one is smiling, all the customers stand with their backs to one another, hands hammer away at knobs and buttons in a frenetic motion. Most striking is the observation that players of video games have the same dull look in their eyes as heavy television watchers.

When pushed for an answer as to why these places are so attractive to children, especially boys, many arcade workers say that these machines are a replacement for loneliness. "Some boys who come in here feel that the arcade is their home," remarks one manager. As the visitor to an arcade looks more closely, he will notice that in most of the games the player shoots things. The machines glorify violence; they are, in fact, electronic war games. Several boys I talked with in Aladdin's Castle at the Nanuet Mall in Nanuet, New York, told me that they feel powerful and in control while playing the games. One boy confessed, "When I'm depressed and angry about something that happened at school, I can come here and shoot away rather than blowing up my history teacher."

Psychiatrists are beginning to see game-fixated youngsters, and they report that for the most part these are disturbed children who dodge reality and human contact. Arcade managers say that their establishments have "regulars," boys who come daily in hopes of increasing their score and thereby being able to place their initials on the video screen of their particular game. Some boys are so addicted they spend upward of $20 a day.

"The incredible thing is that the player keeps depositing quarters, and there's no real reward," one arcade manager told me. "In gambling at least there's a payoff. Here, it is simple recognition. Boys must be awfully hungry for attention to spend all their money for a couple of initials on the screen."

The children most hooked on video games are those with few interests. They don't play sports. They don't participate in extracurricular activities. They actually derive self-esteem from video games. It is possible that the only positive effect of these games is on children with learning problems. According to Robert Jackson, a computer expert and teacher at the Meade School in Westchester, New York, "Children with short attention spans, who are unteachable in most normal school settings can be turned on somewhat by playing with video games and simple computers."[4]

Video games are certainly extensions of the "wired-up" mentality. They are still a novelty and certainly fun to play with on an occasional trip to an arcade, but constant daily doses of these games, like constant television viewing, is inimical to intellectual growth.

If your family is cutting down on television, try to cut down on video games, too. It's all right to play with them, but only after your children have read a book, done something physical, or talked with a friend or family member.

Computers

Parents are often insistent about computer courses in the schools at early levels, and many suburban homes are already equipped with personal computers. There are several public schools in Westchester County, a New York City suburb, where kindergarteners are being introduced to the Logo Computer. This trend toward early exposure carries with it little thought as to what these machines can do to and for children, both mentally and physically, as well as to the learning process itself. It took thirty years to begin to see the effects of television on children, and the effects of computers may similarly require a long time to assess.

If we take into consideration Marie Winn's list of what television *doesn't* do for a child's development, it becomes apparent that computers, put into the hands of children too soon, may also deter certain kinds of significant developmental patterns. Among Winn's points are:

1. Children need to develop capacities for self-direction in order to liberate themselves from dependency. The television experience perpetuates fantasy.
2. Children need to develop fundamental skills in communication— reading, writing, and expression— in order to function as social critics. The television experience does not further verbal development.
3. Children need to discover their own

strengths and weaknesses in order to find fulfillment as adults. Watching television does not lead to self-discovery.

4. Children's needs for fantasy are gratified far better by their own make-believe activities than by adult-made fantasies offered on television.[5]

In every single statement you could substitute the word "computer" for "television." In the formative years the computer, it would seem, creates a dependency on machines rather than on self. Like most electronic devices, computers, in their own good time, may enhance a child's learning experience. But the key words are "enhance" and in "good time."

Educators who believe strongly in the work of Jean Piaget, the French developmental psychologist, acknowledge that steps can't be skipped in the child's mental and physical growth. You can't rush the seasons, they say, and by putting young children in front of machines—televisions, electronic games, computers—too soon, you hamper their growth in the long run. Thomas K. Roney, a teacher of computer science at Kent Preparatory School in Kent, Connecticut, suggests that electronic devices can be used too soon in the educational process. "Questions persist as to whether Johnny's number sense will sink below the nadir reached subsequent to, if not because of, the "new math," and whether his dependence on the calculator will become so great that without it he will be unable to figure a tip or the price of six pencils at twelve cents each. Short-term studies discount this, but there is reason to be wary, particularly if the calculator should induce an ill-considered reduction of arithmetic drills in the lower grades."[6]

Peggy Cole, principal of Fieldston Lower School in Riverdale, New York, and an outspoken critic of television for the young child also questions the appropriateness of computers in the schools. "This educational movement of getting computers into the schools is not coming from an education base but from industry. There is a seduction of technology, tremendous parental pressure and a business motive. What is missing are solid educational reasons for doing it at all. Questions have to be asked first. For example, if you put something into the curriculum, what are you taking out? We usually introduce children to the concrete world in first and second grade before the abstract world. What will it mean to introduce them to the symbolic world first? What about the graphics on computers? Aren't they just as distorting to a child as cartoons?"[7]

At a recent panel on rearing children in the electronic age, one panelist suggested how a computer might be used in class: "Children can plot simulated pioneer trips across the country in a covered wagon, programming in all the hardships they might encounter along the way." The rest of the panelists suggested hands-on activities that could make the same point and make it more compellingly. One panel member mentioned that during deer season a father had brought into school a deer which the children skinned, dried, and stretched, using the experience as part of a pioneer unit they were working on at the time. In other words why simulate an experience on a computer when children can learn from actual experience? "History has shown that teaching devices, when introduced into education, have marginal influence," report William Sharkan and John Goodman. "There is no instructional technology that can substitute completely for a teacher who is a real person— one who has developed an adequate and positive self-concept, who has a system of values, who genuinely likes kids, and who has a desire to teach well."[8]

Like television, computers are here to stay, but they must not be introduced into a child's life, at school or at home, before the child has had time to grasp the basics of education, family life, community life, and his own interests.

Activities in the No-TV Home

Your children won't miss television if they have something equally absorbing to do. After all, generations of children grew up without television. Here are some activities, grouped by age, that you can substitute for television. Build on your children's current interests to make these activities suit your family.

Preschoolers

The hardest children to entertain are often preschoolers because they are home all day. Here are several easy activities that will keep toddlers through six year olds busy, if a little noisy! (Asterisks indicate activities that are explained in detail.)

dolls*	water and bathtub
playing house	play*
simple puzzles	play dough*
rhythm band*	records
coloring, paint-	ball games
ing, drawing	beanbags
simple crafts	block bowling*
leaf piles*	box houses*
hide and seek	paper punching
Simon says	bags*
snow play	masking tape
hike in the house*	roads*
play group*	tumbling mattress
dress up*	cards*

Dolls. Keep a bag full of colorful and silky fabric, rickrack, ribbon, and other trim and old scarves from which your children can create doll clothes. Capes and skirts can be made without sewing.

Rhythm band. Preschoolers love cymbals, triangles, drums, and tambourines. Harmonicas and kazoos are fun, too. For homemade instruments try the following:

- Fill soda bottles to different levels with water. Tap with a spoon for various tones, or blow over the top of the bottles.
- Take a shoe box, and string it with rubber bands to make a harp.
- Fill an empty plastic bottle with a quarter cup of rice. Cover and shake.
- Use an empty oatmeal box as a drum.

Leaf piles. Raking and piling leaves can be fun for everyone. If your children have their own rakes, let them loose to create a leaf fort or a leaf path. For a real treat let children heap the leaves high and trike through the pile. It's also fun for children to jump into leaf piles and bury themselves.

Hike in the house. This is good when other children visit. Have picnic lunches packed for everyone. Children go for a hike through the house pretending that the stairs are "up the mountain." "Past the forest" is through the dining room chairs; "through the city" could be the living room. Finally, arrive at a spot for the picnic. Be sure to clean up the campsite before returning home.

Play group. Join with other parents, and set up a three- or four-child group, rotating houses. For advice see *The Playbook Handbook* by Laura Broad and Nancy Butterworth (St. Martin's Press, 1974).

Dress up. Keep a box full of castoff ties, slips, hats, purses, costume jewelry, scarves, and other accessories. Children can play endlessly dressing up as a favorite character or making up costumes.

Water and bathtub play. Save laundry sprinkles, plastic bottles with squeeze tops, funnels, measuring spoons, sponges, plastic cups, cars, boats, and suction basters for this soothing experience. Preschoolers love water play.

Play dough. This is a must recipe for mothers of all preschool children. Mix one cup of flour with one cup of salt. Add food coloring and enough water to make the dough stiff. Knead until play dough is a good, smooth consistency. Then use rolling pins and cookie cutters, or just make art objects. Afterward, store in a plastic container or a plastic bag.

Block bowling. Set up cardboard boxes at one end of the kitchen floor, and let children roll a rubber ball toward them to see how many boxes they can knock down. A good rainy day sport.

Box houses. Rescue large appliance boxes whenever you see them on the street after delivery of a washing machine or drier. They are perfect for making houses and forts, and children love to have their own private place in the house. Use poster paints for windows and trim.

Paper punching bags. Stuff paper bags or plastic bags with crumped newspapers. Hang the bags from the ceiling, and let children punch them apart until they get tired of this activity.

Masking tape roads. Permit children to design a road around the house and mark it out with masking tape. Children can run cars over their roads.

Cards. Even a young child can play solitaire by putting together all the red cards or all the cards with matching numbers. Kindergartners can arrange the cards in ace-ten sequence. Don't underestimate the entertainment value of a deck of cards.

Bad Day Survival Techniques

In every family there will be days of boredom, rain, sickness, and disappointment or days when parents are especially busy and can't spend too much time with their children. These are the times when television used to come in handy. Here are some suggestions for surprises that can help you through these days.

The comfort bag. Keep a shopping bag filled with manila envelopes that have in them such things as forgotten toys, old pocketbooks filled with junk (supermarket coupons, play money, old keys), stickers and

Scotch tape, playing cards, scissors, costume jewelry, a magnifying glass, magic markers, beeswax, small dolls, a magic slate, paper dolls, marbles, and a harmonica. Let your sad, attention-seeking child pick an envelope or two and work out a good afternoon of play.

The reserved kitchen drawer. Stock a kitchen drawer with junk like a few old kitchen tools and other objects. The selection of objects depends on the age of the child, of course, but this should work for children from eighteen months through kindergarten. Throw in little toys and amusements left behind in the kitchen—badges, cars, magic balls, string, popsicle sticks—so they're right where you need them, especially on days when you're stuck in the kitchen.

The surprise box. Have a box hidden away into which you put toys picked up on sale, coloring and activity books, crayons, packs of baseball cards, miniatures for doll houses, yo-yos, and other items to perk up and keep a child busy. The surprise box shouldn't be overworked, or it will become a bribe. Keep it as an emergency measure. The surprise box can be adapted for all ages.

Elementary School Children

Six to ten year olds often have scheduled after-school activities, and some may have homework or instrument practice. Here's a list to supplement the regular round of activities.

reading	letter writing (pen
tin foil baseball*	pal program)
Nerf football	bike riding
basement bowling	baseball card flip
ball games	solitaire
darts	board games with
newspaper war*	siblings or friends
holiday crafts	jump rope
meal prepara-	acorn fights*
tion*	hopscotch
woodworking*	weekly library
crafts*	visits
skateboarding	flashlight tag*
rollerskating	collection or hobby
tag	kite flying
pet care	jacks

Tin foil baseball. This is a helpful game when real baseball can't be played. Crumple up tin foil to make a small ball, and bat it with a stick. No harm done, lots of fun, and nothing gets broken.

Newspaper war. Make balls out of crumpled newspapers. Suggest a war when the children have been shut in for a few days and need to do something wild and aggressive.

Meal preparation. At this age a child can be very helpful around dinner time setting the table, peeling carrots, breaking up salad. This is also a good way to spend some

time with the parent who is making the
meal.

Woodworking. Hammers, nails, blocks
of wood, sandpaper, vices, screws, and screw
drivers will keep any child happy for a good
length of time. Suggest that your child make
wooden sculptures or model houses or just
practice hammering.

Crafts. Wooden wine crates and grape
boxes make marvelous doll houses and forts
for soldiers. Likewise, orange crates make
nice bedside tables. If you are the start-
from-scratch type, visit your local lumber-
yard and pick up supplies for building book-
cases or shelves. Designing, sawing, nailing,
sanding and painting are all great activities
for the industrious child.

Acorn fights. Cut out cardboard shields.
Let the children collect a pile of acorns and
fight away.

Flashlight tag. A good substitute for a
favorite prime-time TV program is flashlight tag. It is played outside at night. The
person who is "it" has a flashlight; when he
shines the light on someone, that person is
caught.

Junior High Schoolers

At this age children often have a busy
schedule, and it's easy to overlook family
activities and hobbies that can lay the foundation for a lifelong interest.

reading
model building
on-going games*
challenging
 puzzles*
journal
movie going
stamp or coin
 collecting
cooking
team sports

jogging
after-school Y
 program
getting in shape
chores
clubs
earning pocket
 money*
volunteer
 activities*

On-going games. Set aside time after dinner, a few nights a week, to play time-consuming games such as Monopoly. You can continue the same game nightly for a week if need be. You'll be practically bankrupt on Tuesday and recover your losses on Thursday! Various word and card games, chess, and checkers also can be played on this basis. Keep a weekly score.

Challenging puzzles. Here's a lost treat. A started puzzle on a card table is an enticing activity for a long winter evening. Leave the puzzle out until it's finished. Anyone can drop by any time to fit in a piece.

Earning pocket money. At this age children can start earning pocket money by doing chores in the neighborhood—walking dogs, raking leaves, babysitting. If you want your children to do some extra chores around the house beyond their regular assignments, you might consider paying them a small wage to rake leaves, help clean up the backyard, and so on.

Volunteer activities. As children approach their teens, they can investigate some of the volunteer activities in the neighborhood at hospitals and senior citizen centers and through church- and school-organized groups.

These suggestions are meant to get you started in alternate activities. They are only a small sample of the possibilities your children will enjoy. You'll surely discover many more. Here are a few books that are entertaining and helpful in suggesting many new avenues to explore.

Peter Cardozo, *The 3rd Whole Kids' Catalog* (Bantam, 1981).

Susan Striker, *The 4th Anti-Coloring Book* (Holt, Rinehart and Winston, 1980). There are also three earlier volumes.

Alan Rose, *Build Your Own Eiffel Tower* (Perigree, 1981). Other "build your own" titles are *Build Your Own Tower Bridge, Guillotine, Titanic, U.S. Capitol,* and *Windmill.*

Jean Marzollo and Janice Loyd, *Learning Through Play* (Harper-Colophon, 1972).

Charles Wolfgang, Bea MacKener, and Mary Wolfgang, *Growing and Learning Through Play* (McGraw-Hill, 1981).

S. Adams Sullivan, *The Father's Almanac* (Doubleday, 1980).

Platt Monfort, *Styro-Flyers—How to Build Super Model Planes from Hamburg Boxes and Other Fast-Food Containers* (Random House, 1981).

Your local bookstore and library can offer many more good suggestions.

Adult Viewing Problems

One of the many problems families encounter when they try to cut down on television is that the parents, not the children, may be the serious viewers. So often the children would just as soon have the television set off and their parents available to them instead, but their parents have too heavy a TV habit to break easily. The Four-Week Program should be a big help, but for parents with a special interest—sports, news, soap operas—here are a few suggestions.

Sports Freak

There once was an eight-year-old boy named Henry. He hated football, or so he said to his mother. One bright fall day his mother happened to gaze out the window, and there was Henry, playing football with his father. After the game she remarked, "I

thought you told me that you hated football, Henry." "Oh," said the boy with a grin,
"I hate to watch football, but I love to play
it."

After hearing this story, many fathers
make a conscious effort to play a bit more
with their children rather than leaving all
the sports action to the television.

Television sports has changed marriages, family life, and major holidays.
Thanksgiving dinner is arranged so it
doesn't coincide with a football game;
Easter dinner is usually interrupted by the
Masters Golf Tournament. Television sports
have taken active fathers and made them
into passive spectators. The advent of cable
and sports channels will only increase the
possibilities for watching instead of participating.

Here are some tips for controlling sports
viewing:

1. Treat television sports the same way
   you treat a live sports event which
   you buy tickets for. If you buy tickets to a soccer, baseball, or football
   game, you plan to attend one event.
   Choose to watch one major event, not
   an entire day of televised events.
2. For every sporting event you watch
   on television play in one game of
   your chosen sport.
3. To repay family time for time spent
   watching a sports event, participate

with family members in a casual game of catch, football, frisbee, whatever.

4. Remind yourself that activity, not passivity, lengthens life and keeps the cardiovascular system healthy. Cardiologists believe that, in part, passive television viewing accounts for the sharp increase in heart disease among younger men.

News Freaks

Defending their habit people frequently tell me, "I only watch the news." My answer is in the form of a question: "How much news?"

The news shows on television are fast becoming the medium's most popular form of entertainment. In large metropolitan areas a viewer can watch eighteen hours of news programming on Saturday and Sundays and as much as twenty-seven hours during the week. Add to these staggering figures magazine-type programs such as "20/20" and "Sixty Minutes," and the viewer can accumulate not only large doses of daily news but be informed on every conceivable background or feature story.

But are you really being fully informed by watching those endless rounds of news shows? Don Bresnahan, a producer of television news documentaries, explains TV this way.

> *To the vast majority of news-hungry Americans . . . TV news offers all the news they want, all the news they think they need.*
>
> *This, perhaps, is the greatest sin of TV news; it has conditioned people to believe that what we have shown and told them is THE NEWS. It isn't, and everyone writing, reporting, editing, directing, producing and anchoring knows it isn't.*
>
> *We are in the headline business. We are in the tip-of-the-iceberg business. We pretend, in our own defense, that we are only whetting your appetite, and firmly insist that when you have finished viewing one of our local or network newscasts, you should rush out and buy a printed source for the rest of the story. We are guilty of giving you too little because we are desperately afraid that you really don't want any more.*[9]

With this in mind it may be easier to break the news addiction, especially for people who want time for family talk, at dinner and in the evening. The family will surely benefit more from discussion of a news event than from a television broadcast. Try these simple rules:

1. Choose one half hour of television news a day. Test a few programs

until you find the one that serves you best, and watch just that one.

2. If you feel you must watch the national news at 7 o'clock, do so with a small portable away from young children. If your children are in the upper elementary grades, watch with them, ready to explain stories that may seem confusing or frightening.

3. Replace morning television news with radio news.

4. Subscribe to one good comprehensive newspaper, and read it thoroughly. You will not only get a broader picture of the story, but sometimes several points of view.

5. So you don't feel out of touch with world events and trends, during the weaning process watch PBS's "Washington Week in Review."

6. If you must watch more than one news show a day, choose a second show after the children are in bed.

Soap Opera Addict

Perhaps the hardest habit to control is watching television soap operas, also known as daily serials. The story line is written to entice the addicted viewer to tune in tomorrow and tomorrow and tomorrow. The characters on the soaps are particularly entertaining, and many find it both fun and

stimulating to live vicariously through their
favorite stars as an escape from domestic
drudgery.

However, there are some real draw-
backs to soap opera addiction.

1. The shows are on when children are
   up and round, and the sexual ex-
   plicitness as well as the tragic story
   lines can be upsetting to small children. Once I was a "Search for Tomorrow" addict. Years later my
   children asked what happened to one
   of the young characters who had lost
   his parents and had no real home life.
2. Being stuck on a soap or several
   soaps means daily watching. Children learn by example, and mothers
   aren't setting a very good one by
   avoiding other activities so they can
   watch *their* programs. Many women
   won't take their children to the park
   during soap time. They take the
   phone off the hook and refuse to
   schedule activities that interfere
   with the soap schedule.
3. Many lonely housewives feel let down
   directly after watching their daily
   soap opera. The compulsive need to
   see the show is never satisfied by the
   show itself. This feeling will effect
   your children. They will also believe
   that TV characters are real and
   meaningful.

Breaking away from soap operas is not easy, but success stories abound. Here are some pointers:

1. Begin easing away from your favorite show by watching only Monday and Friday. You will get all the story line information you need during those two days.
2. Supplement the story line, if needed, by reading the weekly plot in the newspaper.
3. Plan to be out of the house while your soap is on the air. Plan a scheduled activity such as a tennis game or a hairdresser appointment so that you must attend.
4. If you need the escapism that soap operas provide, read a good romantic novel.
5. Set a time limit after which you will cut out seeing the Monday segment of your soap; two weeks after cut out Friday.

What to Expect When Your Home Is TV Free

Expect a higher noise level. On weekend mornings you'll probably hear balls bouncing, water swishing, doors slamming, and music playing. The consolation prize is that the new sounds are friendlier and more pleasant than the deadening beat of cartoons.

Expect a messier house. Children busy at play make messes which, of course, they can learn to clean up. They like to play near their parents when they are inside, which means a messy kitchen and family room. They enjoy bringing worms, caterpillars, and lost treasures to the kitchen door to show them off. This means dirt tracked inside, but it's all in the name of good healthy play!

Expect a more active household. Children who are not tucked away in front of a TV screen are running in and out, jumping off ledges, hopping, climbing, and, with all this, falling, bleeding, and crying. Generally they are involved, very happy, and very tired at the end of the day.

Expect more demands. Children will want to go to the library or the bookstore. They'll ask to be chauffeured to friends' houses, and they'll want to have friends over to sleep. They will start huge collections of rocks, animals, coins, or stamps—all of which will mean you'll have to supply some time, some money, and some patience.

Expect to spend money. You'll find yourself buying sports equipment and craft projects, and paying for some library fines as well as tickets for movies, excursions to bowling alleys, and skating rinks. One consolation is that these expenses will no doubt be far cheaper than your electric bills for television overuse. Older children, however, can start earning the money for their new hobbies by doing special chores—walking the dog, cleaning the cat box, raking the leaves, working for neighbors.

Expect the return of some of your favorite things. This includes calm children, husbands not in front of the tube all weekend, old-fashioned family life, and more time for everyone and everything.

Expect permanent changes in your children. Unlike lung damage from too much cigarette smoking or liver disease from too much drinking, the damages incurred from too much television are repairable. Many of the symptoms of TV abuse will simply disappear with the disappearance of TV viewing.

Take the demand for toys and foods advertised on television, for example. Less-TV mothers boast of a certain smugness that comes while Christmas and birthday shopping. "The demands from the children are less," they report. "There I stand being creative in the toy store of all places. I go up and down the aisles looking for surprises, things my kids don't even know exist because they don't see commercials anymore."

Being responsible for their own entertainment also slows children down and makes them more patient. They no longer have to have what they want *right now*!

Parties, creative play, sporting skills (new adventures for many ex-TV addicts) lead to organized thought. No longer is everything instant, like the flick of the TV button, and as time goes on, children without television develop a respect for process, for things that take time.

Back to their own individual rhythms, children who are off television wake up in more ways than one. They play at their own pace, deeply yet energetically involved. Observe televisionless children at play. They are often more systematic and organized than TV watchers. No longer in a hurry to "change channels" or get to the next "program," they can spend hours creating a roadway with blocks or making up their own adventures.

Junk food doesn't disappear unless parents make it go away. However, without the insistent demands from television ordering the child to purchase one thing or another, the urge to buy such products does begin to diminish.

Mothers rarely report hearing "I'm bored" when the television is gone. Many children's interests move on to musical instruments, hands-on projects, and organized sports. These activities leave little time to be bored.

Good conversation regenerates in televisionless homes. There is now time to really listen to one another around the dinner table and into the evening hours. Children regain some of their powers of focus and concentration. Those who were previously inarticulate and inattentive have a chance to practice talking and listening again. Gradually their thought patterns and sentence structure lose the jagged, hesitant flavor of TV talk, and language becomes less painful and smoother. Nightmares are often replaced with pleasant dreams as storytelling becomes part of the bedtime ritual.

Not only are negative aspects of TV eliminated once a family has decided on less television, but there are now more important, positive goals that can be achieved. The most worthy of these, perhaps, is providing situations and an environment for family members, especially children, to develop into whole people. A whole person is mentally, physically, spiritually, and emotionally alive. If a person, adult or child, has given over a large portion of his time to television, it becomes impossible for him to develop fully. By participating in activities that will develop each aspect of the personality you are stimulating one part or another of yourself and thus growing no matter what your age.

Remember, there are worthwhile goals to be achieved once a family is on the course of less television. The most worthy of these, perhaps, is providing situations and an environment for family members to become whole people again. Looking at the diagram below will help you understand this goal and provide a framework in which to work.

Whole Person

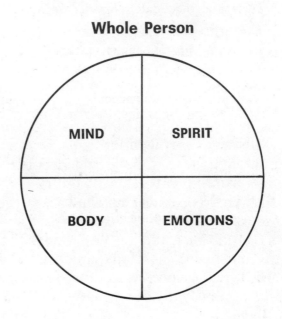

Notes

1. Patricia Williams, Edward Haertel, Geneva Haertel, and Herbert Walberg, "The Impact of Leisure-Time Television on School Learning: A Research Synthesis," *American Educational Research Journal*, Spring 1982, p. 35.

2. Switch, The Children's Television Game, is available through ACT, Action for Children's Television, 46 Austin Street, Newtonville, Massachusetts 02160.

3. Jerome L. Singer and Dorothy G. Singer, "Is Human Imagination Going Down the Tube?"

Chronicle of Higher Education, April 23, 1979, p. 30.

4. Remarks made at a panel discussion sponsored by the Fox Meadow Parent-Teachers Association, Scarsdale, New York, March 8, 1982.

5. Marie Winn, *The Plug-In Drug*, Bantam, 1978, p. 7.

6. "The Computer as Cornucopia in Education," *Kent Literary Magazine*, Spring 1982, p. 10.

7. Quoted by Sally Reed, "Schools Enter the Computer Age," *New York Times Spring Survey of Education*, April 25, 1982.

8. William Sharkan, and John Goodman, "The Microcomputer in Education: Myth or Panacea?" *Media and Management Journal*, Winter 1982, pp. 26–27, 35.

9. "My Turn," *Newsweek*, April 19, 1982, p. 23.

7
THE JOYS
OF
BEING LIVE

Staying unplugged is not deprivation. In fact, many families report that after their decision to live without television or with a very limited amount, they feel free for the first time from the dictatorial hold television had had on their lives.

What follows are the stories of several families: the Eatons, who never had television to begin with; the McKays, who followed the Four-Week No-TV Program; and the Rolfes and Bennisons, both of whom participated in a no-television program sponsored by their children's schools.

The Eatons

The Eaton family has been living with little or no television for almost fifteen years. Hidden in the corner, under a desk in the dining room of their home in Spring Valley, New York, is a dusty old television set. It remains there on purpose. At least three members of the Eaton family feel they are candidates for TV addiction; they want the television out of convenient reach.

Chuck and Anne Eaton have three children, Claire, who is eighteen years old, Willie, who is fifteen, and Chandra, who is eleven. Anne teaches music and English, and Chuck is a psychologist at Roosevelt Hospital in New York City.

"Television isn't a forbidden fruit," says Chuck, "but Anne doesn't believe in it for children so when they started coming along, we had to make a decision about our viewing habits." The Eatons watched television about three times last year. "We turned it on for the Super Bowl," explains Chuck, "and promptly the electricity went out. We watched the ball come down in Times Square on New Year's Eve, and I don't remember the third time."

Chuck arrived at his television consciousness by figuring out what television did to him. He would come home every night with papers to do. Anne, alone all day with the children, wanted to talk. The children also demanded his attention. In response to this, Chuck would turn on any old program and not do anything.

"I never liked TV, so it wasn't hard for me to stop watching," says Anne. "And I felt it was wrong for babies to be watching. Have you ever really looked at a child in front of the tube? The poor thing looks like he's had the child knocked out of him. It's unnatural for a child, until he is about seven, to be anything but active and busy."

So rather than be done to, as Anne phrased the watching of television, the Eatons started doing for themselves. They kept a diary for a week to log the typical activities of a family who doesn't watch television. Heavy snow days had them all together for a few days in and out of the house. Two hours on Saturday morning were spent bird watching. Outside the children built snow forts, which ended up taking two days. The entire family went sledding and tobogganing. All the Eatons play musical instruments, so it seemed there was always some group or individual playing. Breakfasts and dinners were all sit-down affairs with everyone together. Sandwiched between the fun were the weekly chores of bread baking, food coop work, Bach Society for Anne, Suburban Symphony for Chuck, babysitting for Claire and Willie, two sleepover's for Chandra, and a great deal of reading.

The Eatons are content with their life. "Let's say," says Chuck, "that at the end of the year I remember the concerts we attended, the people we met, and some shining family treks more than I would remember the television season."

The McKays

Everywhere you look in the Jim McKay household in Pearl River, New York, there is a television staring at you. And yet, Edith was determined to make her family more conscious of the television in their lives. The family methodically proceeded through the Four-Week No-TV Program, and what they realized when they came to Week Four follows.

There are six McKays. Two children are away at college, leaving fourteen-year-old Kathy and sixteen-year-old Tom home with Jim and Edith McKay. Jim commutes to New York City, where he works on Wall Street, while Edith holds down the fort, running a wild, busy household with a constant stream of teenagers coming and going.

Explaining Week Four Edith says, "The house suddenly became very quiet, almost as if there had been a death or a good friend was missing. We immediately resurrected several radios from the basement, and I got reacquainted with my favorite talk radio station."

Jim's preference is to listen to the radio news anyway. He says his life was unaffected that first day until evening came and he automatically flicked on the tube. "No, no, Dad," reminded Tom. Jim settled down to a crossword puzzle.

Kathy McKay noticed one annoying thing during that first quiet week—her father's classical music. "Yuk!" was her comment.

"We all came together and felt closer," says Edith. "Everyone is in on everyone else's business when the TV is not there. That first week we observed the changes in our habits. I guess families tend to stop listening and watching each other if they always have a TV on. We were no exception."

"It is different all right," chimes in Jim with a chuckle. "With less TV there is a lot more mid-week chauffeuring for me. Tommy costs me more money—the movies, visiting friends, and talking long distance on the phone."

"We started this experiment in the winter," says Kathy, "when I was always much more tempted to watch a movie or game show. Instead now I get to clean out the basement, study harder for exams, chop wood, and shovel snow!"

She really wasn't complaining that much, her mother explained. "Her grades have improved immeasurably this term, and I think it has to do with Kathy's taking more time and being more thorough."

Edith realized that more free time for herself meant a new-found interest in creating some good meals. She also began to get out in the morning. "No dawdling over the 'Today Show.' " Instead she scheduled her paddle ball game to a new early hour.

But there were some dismal times that first week. The McKays continued to pull out the television page from the newspaper to see what was on. One night Kathy saw an ad for a special and wished she could see it. In fact, as a sort of protest she went to a friends house and watched the program. Jim was out of town one night, and Edith said she missed the tradition of the children gathering in her room to watch a few shows together. Instead, everyone was scattered. "Five o'clock was the grimmest," recalls Edith. "It's the time of day I least like, and I had always filled in that gap with the news."

Initially, the kids said they knew something else was missing but couldn't quite put their finger on it. Finally, Tommy realized it was junk food. "We used to eat lots of munchie stuff in the evening. In fact, there were half hourly gatherings in the kitchen when we used to all meet between shows to grab some food and find out what everyone else was up to."

"Now our hands are full of busy-type things—books, magazines, needlepoint, and projects," says Edith.

Kathy, a sport nut, doubles her time on the basketball court these days. She also reports sleeping longer and better. "I need more sleep than I used to get," she admits. "Tommy and I have nothing to stay up late for, especially on Saturday nights, with the television control in this house."

Edith concurs and says that she no longer gets a TV hangover. "You know the feeling, don't you?—when you watch TV until you fall asleep. It can't be good for a restful night's sleep. I do sleep better now that the TV is out of the bedroom."

"We had always been a close family, but television was beginning to rear its ugly head," Jim says. "We were shutting each other out. We pick and choose carefully these days, using television after other possibilities are exhausted."

The Rolfes

After several years of talking to and counseling parents on how to turn off the TV sets, I decided to go to the children themselves and began presenting No-TV Week programs in schools. Many families' lives have been dramatically altered after their children participated in these programs. The children are enthusiastic and learn a great deal about a medium they once took for granted. In many cases, their parents are less excited. Some find that they cannot break their addiction to television. But many, with the help of their children and for the good of their children, are beginning to try.

Life has changed dramatically in the household of Sondra and Trevor Rolfe since their children participated in a No-TV Week Program at school.

"We've cut out early morning TV altogether," says Sondra. Peter, age seven, has always been an early riser and has been watching in the morning his entire life. I never really approved, but what else was he going to do when the rest of the house was still asleep? But morning TV slowed him down; he was always dragging his body and was continuously late for school. Morning TV is something he chose to eliminate. In its place I get a little boy in our bed for a longer morning cuddle."

The most addicted member of the Rolfe household was Trevor, who agreed to go along with No-TV Week while the children were up. The first night Trevor Rolfe kept to his plan of no television until the children were bedded down. "The minute they were settled, the TV went on," reports Sondra. "However, on Night 2 I felt a tiny sense of victory. After the kids were in bed he opted for a book and conversation with me."

In an effort to convert their father, Peter and Allison, age eleven spent time after dinner tackling him on the couch, engaging him in conversation, showing them their school work, and getting some reaction. "He didn't know what was happening," Sondra reports, "but the kids were reaching out and Trevor was reciprocating." When Trevor did watch his usual dose of weekend sports, Peter and Allison would not go near him for fear of breaking their No-TV Week pledge.

Sondra grew up in South Africa, and when she came to the United States, she was surprised and saddened that she seldom saw anyone outside, at least in the suburbs. Her feelings got a boost during No-TV Week. "The street was full of kids, everyone doing something. The bikes were out, wagons were carting junk, basketballs were bouncing, Nerf football catches were going on the front lawn. It was like a three-ring circus."

Sondra noticed that the neighborhood children needed one another more when television was out of the picture. "It was apparent to me that No-TV Week brought the kids together both in spirit and physically. It brought the community out of the closet and into each other's homes. I don't want to sound Pollyanna-ish. Everything wasn't terrific. There was a lot of noise—excited kids, people coming and going, so much talk, talk, talking. Sometimes at the end of the day I longed to be just sitting quietly in front of the TV. Another problem, if you could call playing, talking, and the like, a problem, was the mess. The children set up little retreats in every corner of the house. There wasn't a blanket or sheet in the linen closet. Once inside these little retreats, the children read, talked, played with their Legos and Matchboxes, and had fun."

One interesting note from the Rolfe household is that the children didn't gravitate to games. "They gravitated to each other and me," says Sondra. She is particularly excited about Allison's new found hobby—reading. Never an ardent reader prior to No-TV Week, Allison has now taken to reading frequently and to choosing books to read to her younger brother.

After one week of No-TV the Rolfes learned that they definitely can live without television. The TV set had not been turned on by Sondra or a child for three weeks after the school program, except for one night. "I caught Peter watching a space documentary," said Sondra. "When I walked in on him, he jumped from his seat and yelled, 'It's all right! It's all right! I've done all my work, and this is a good, short show.' "

The Bennisons

"I only watched two hours of television last week," exclaimed nine-year-old Vanessa Bennison, as if she had accomplished a major feat. Vanessa's family had participated in her school's No-TV Week and as an ongoing project, Vanessa pledged to watch no more than two hours a week for the remainder of the school year. In fact, all the members of the Bennison household feel good about themselves several weeks after participating in No-TV Week.

Leslie Bennison, the mother of Vanessa

and Dana, age five, is especially happy to
see the trickle-down effect occurring with
other family members. "Dana, our preschooler, is not a self-starter. With no neighborhood children in her age group, television
had become Dana's best friend. During No-
TV Week, however, with her sister busy at
projects and me generating play ideas, Dana
began to leave television behind and gravitate to where the action was. TV seems no
longer to be where it's at. I suppose the week
was a real eye-opener in other ways," reveals Leslie. "An anti-TV program *must*
involve the entire family. A parent can't
just yell at the kids and tell them to turn
the set off. I was forced to take a real position against television, as well as take an
active part in organizing everyone's time.
At times, I must have sounded like a broken
record—'Get out the magic markers,' 'Build
a castle.' The house sure looks different with
little snippets of paper strewn around and
paste stuck to the kitchen table, but there is
also some maternal satisfaction."

The Bennisons were never what you
would call an addicted family. However,
Leslie was on the road to TV addiction when
the girls were babies and her husband Bill
was traveling half the year. "Back then I
was watching TV day and night, slowly falling into a real trap. I began to realize that
TV had almost a hypnotic effect on me,
drawing me to it for no reason. Finally one
afternoon I simply turned the darn thing

off. I wasn't living my life anymore. I was living *their* life—the television characters!" The big bone of contention in the Bennison household is one that exists in many homes: Bill Bennison has a sports addiction. "I must admit if I didn't travel so much I might be tempted to tune into the HBO sporting events every evening. Some of my male friends watch two or three sporting matches a night." In his defense, Bill asserts that during No-TV Week he probably clocked only two hours of sports. "On Friday night," he reminds his wife with a grin, "we were forced to do a real family number. It's rare that the four of us are ever together, alone. That night we popped popcorn and had a wild game of Concentration and Scrabble. I found myself thinking how good it felt, the whole family around the card table."

Leslie thinks that television makes men age a lot faster. "I think all the passive watching, especially for men, makes them sedentary and old looking." No-TV Week provided the perfect opportunity for her to chide Bill about his lack of exercise and lawn mowing.

Did the Bennisons' No-TV Week produce any lasting effects? "Oh yes, indeed," says Leslie. "We have absolutely no television now during the week. We are superconscious now of available extra time and fill it up with more productive alternatives. The other night Vanessa finished her home-

work with ten minutes to spare before dinner. Instead of the easy out—TV—she went
for a quick bike ride. Best of all, the house
is calm. Even though there is increased activity, the noise level seems toned down.
Everyone seems more relaxed, and I hope to
keep it that way."

After a family begins to cut down on
television viewing, a certain chain of events
usually occurs.

1. The entire family will be forced to
   learn information—local, national,
   and international news and day to
   day trivia—from sources other than
   television.
2. Family members will also be forced
   to get their entertainment and pleasure from other people—family
   members, friends, and themselves.
3. The two situations mentioned above
   make for one very immediate result
   —more talk.
4. The next surprise is more time—big
   blocks of free, unprogramed time,
   which means less household tension
   and no hurrying of meals to make a
   program.
5. Lack of tension breeds breathing
   space—time to just sit and relax and
   perhaps linger over a conversation,
   happening, or special moment.
6. Lingering time means children who

bask in new-found attention. Children begin to exhibit the first signs of relief that the television is gone.
7. Then what follows is a surprise for parents—the realization that their children know how to play and that parents don't have to be on duty programing play constantly.

Life takes on an entirely new meaning. With no electronic constraints, many free-from-TV families experience, for the first time, the joys of being themselves and of having the time to develop their own interests.

8
CHANNELING
YOUR
FUTURE

As I conclude this book, the baseball season is upon us. I trudge out to our local Little League field every couple of days to root my son's team on. The children look like normal, healthy youngsters and they are. However, their coaches tell me that they are a different breed from their counterparts of five to ten years ago. I overheard one coach say, "The boys don't hustle. They act as if they are beaten. It's as if they've had the spunk and fight knocked out of them." Another coach agreed, "Many of the boys are downright passive, as if they're in a daze."

We are dealing with a new child today. Television has stifled his growth. If a child watches cartoons before a Saturday morning baseball game, isn't he likely to be logy by the time he arrives for the game? If he spends afternoons and late spring evenings in an armchair instead of in the yard, isn't he likely to be slow, clumsy, and physically undeveloped? If a child has spent the better part of his early years being entertained instead of entertaining himself, being talked to instead of talking, being told television stories instead of reading stories, isn't he likely to grow up lifeless instead of lifelike? A nine year old from San Francisco summed up the attitude of these children: "I'd rather watch TV than play outside because it's boring outside."

Parents are the ones in the driver's seat. In the end only they can determine their children's development and attitudes toward life. As a parent, I want to be the one to establish my children's values, attitudes, and tastes. I want to show them the whole world, not just an artificial slice of TV life.

With controlled television viewing the job of bringing up your children the way you desire is enormously simplified. You will be the one to formulate what is really important to you and to your children. Do you want children who are self-motivated, who read, and who enjoy participating in family events, school projects, and sports? Do you want bubbly, enthusiastic children? Do you want children who are individuals, who prefer to set their own styles?

By controlling television viewing you can begin to achieve these goals. Less television in your household marks the beginning of a richer life, free of commercial interruption and electronic intrusion. Eunice Shriver, the mother of five and executive vice president of the Joseph P. Kennedy Foundation, says, "What the American family needs most of all is a new sense of its own importance, a new definition of its indispensable role, and the reminder of the wonder and delight which should be part of discovering one another and sharing in the amazing unfolding of the mind and body of the child."[1]

With less television your child will be the benefactor of a richer life through books, art, and creative play. He will be the source of his own entertainment, and he will discover his own resources. He will learn from the whole range of human experience and be able to choose his own pathway more intelligently.

"Childhood is so brief," said the poet Walter de la Mare, "and yet so open and formative. Impressions are taken into maturity. I cannot believe that children exposed to the best of literature will later choose that which is cheap and demeaning. That is why only the best is good enough for children for whom we are shaping a future."[2]

By turning off television, we are forced to nourish neglected hemispheres of the brain, the body, and the spirit. I hope I have not created the impression that by eliminating or cutting down on television viewing all the problems of children's growth and development will be solved. Rather, I'm suggesting that by cutting back on television we make a beginning toward finding the special needs of each child and his family. We are clearing up the environment—the electronic environment—and replacing it with a clean slate on which each child and each family can begin to draw their own futures.

Notes

1. "Family Play: A Source of Joy and Growth," *Let's Celebrate the Family*, American Mothers Committee, 1976, p. 18.

2. *Bells and Grass*, Viking, 1964.

BIBLIOGRAPHY

ADLER, RICHARD. "Parents' Television Guide."
Learning, the Magazine for Creative Teaching,
supplement, December 1978.
Annenberg School of Communications. "A Ten
Year Study of TV Violence," 1979.
ARLEN, MICHAEL. *The View from Highway 1.*
New York: Farrar, Straus & Giroux, 1976.
BANDURA, ALBERT, D. ROSS, and S. A. ROSS. "Imi-
tation of Film-Mediated Aggressive Models."
Journal of Abnormal and Social Psychology,
1963, pp. 3–11.
BETTELHEIM, BRUNO. *The Informed Heart.* New
York: The Free Press, 1960.
———. *The Uses of Enchantment—The Meaning
and Importance of Fairy Tales.* New York:
Knopf, 1978.
BRONFENBRENNER, URIE. "Who Lives on Sesame
Street?" *Psychology Today,* October 1970, pp.
14–18, 20.
COHEN, DOROTHY. "Is TV a Pied Piper?" *Young
Children Journal,* November 1974, pp. 4–12.
COHEN, MARCIA. "How Do Prominent Parents
Govern Their Children's TV Habits?" *New
York Times,* March 30, 1980.

ELKIND, DAVID. *The Hurried Child—Growing Up Too Fast Too Soon.* Reading, Mass.: Addison Wesley, 1981.

FAIST, RUSS. "Here's How to Handle TV." *Catholic Universe Bulletin,* September 29, 1978.

Federal Communications Commission. *Report on the Broadcast of Violent, Indecent, Obscene Material.* Washington, D.C., Government Printing Office, 1975.

FEINBLOOM, RICHARD I. "Television and Children." *Ambulatory Pediatric Association,* vol. 13, no. 1 (1977), pp. 11–14.

FILL, HERBERT. "The Mental Breakdown of the Nation." *New Viewpoints,* 1973.

FISKE, EDWARD. "College Entry Tests Drop Sharply." *New York Times,* September 7, 1975.

GEIGER, KENT, and ROBERT SOKOL. "Social Norms in Television Watching." *American Journal of Sociology,* vol. 65 (1959), pp. 174–181.

GOLDSEN, ROSE K. *The Show and Tell Machine— How Television Works and Works You Over.* New York: Delta, 1978.

HALPERN, WERNER I. "Turned-on Toddlers—The Effects of Television on Children and Adolescents." *Journal of Communications,* vol. 25 (Autumn 1975), pp. 66–70.

HARTLEY, E. L. "Passive Learning from Television." *Public Opinion Quarterly,* vol. 34 (1970), pp. 184–190.

HIMMELWEIT, HILDA T., A. N. OPPENHEIM, and PAMELA VINCE. *Television and the Child.* London: Oxford University Press, 1958.

HIRSCH, ELIZABETH S. "TV and the Child Under Six." *New York Early Education Reporter,* Winter 1979, p. 3.

KENISTON, KENNETH. *All Our Children: The American Family Under Pressure.* New York: Harcourt Brace Jovanovich, 1977.

KEY, WILSON BRYAN. *Media Sexploitation.* New York: Signet, 1976.

KRUGMAN, HERBERT E. "Brain Waves Measures of Media Involvement." *Journal of Advertising Research,* February 1971, pp. 3–9.

————. "Processes Underlying Exposure to Advertising." *American Psychologist*, vol. 23 (1968), pp. 245–253.

"Laboratory Investigation of Effects of Television on Children." *TC Today* (newsletter of Teachers College, Columbia University), vol. 10 (Fall 1981), pp. 4–5.

LEONARD, JOHN. "Reflections of My Seven Years at Sword's Point." *New York Times*, April 17, 1977.

LESSER, GERALD S. *Children and Television*. New York: Random House, 1974.

MAEROFF, GENE I. "Specific TV Shows Tied to Child's Achievement." *New York Times*, March 30, 1982.

MANDER, JERRY. *Four Arguments for the Elimination of Television*. New York: Morrow, 1978.

MARIANI, JOHN. "The Impact of TV Violence on Your Children." *Family Weekly*, November 11, 1979, p. 32.

MAYER, MARTIN. *About Television*. New York: Harper and Row, 1972.

MONACO, JAMES. *Media Culture*. New York: Delta, 1978.

MOODY, KATE. "The Research on TV—A Disturbing Picture." *New York Times*, April 20, 1980.

PEARL, DAVID. *Television and Behavior: 10 Years of Scientific Progress and Implications for the Eighties*. Washington, D.C., Government Printing Office, 1982.

POSTMAN, NEIL. "Order in the Classroom." *Atlantic Monthly*, September 1979, pp. 35–38.

————. "TV's Disastrous Impact on Children." *U.S.News and World Report*, January 19, 1981, pp. 43–46.

ROGERS, VINCENT R., and JOAN BARON. "Declining Test Scores: A Humanistic Explanation." *Phi Delta Kappan*, December 1976, pp. 83–86.

SCHRAMM, WILLIAM, JACK LYLE, and EDWIN B. PARKER. *Television in the Lives of Our Children*. Stanford, Calif.: Stanford University Press, 1961.

SINGER, JEROME L., and DOROTHY G. "Is Human

Imagination Going Down the Tube?" *Chronicle of Higher Education*, April 23, 1979.

———. "Television, a Member of the Family." *The National Elementary Principal Magazine*, vol. 6 (January/February 1977), pp. 50–53.

Television and Social Behavior, a Technical Report to the Surgeon General's Scientific Advisory Commission on Television and Social Behavior, 5 vols. Washington, D.C., Government Printing Office, 1972.

WATERS, HARRY. "What TV Does to Kids." *Newsweek*, February 21, 1977, pp. 63–70.

WILKINS, JOAN. "Why Is This Child Always Watching?" *Family Health*, September 1981, pp. 39–40, 58, 60.

———. "The FC Guide." *Family Circle*, April 22, 1980, pp. 20, 24, 52, 54.

———. "A Hard Look at the Tube." *Journal News* (Rockland County, N.Y.), February 20–23, 1978.

WILLIAMS, PATRICIA, EDWARD HAERTEL, GENEVA HAERTEL, and HERBERT WALBERG. "The Impact of Leisure-Time Television on School Learning: A Research Synthesis." *American Educational Research Journal*, vol. 19, no. 1 (Spring 1982).

WINN, MARIE. *The Plug-In Drug*. New York: Viking Press, 1977; Bantam, 1978.

INDEX